D1716003

Todd Wehr Memorial Library
Viterbo College—La Crosse, WI

CHRISTIAN HUMANISM
A Critique of the Secular City
and It's Ideology

CHRISTIAN HUMANISM
A Critique of the Secular City and It's Ideology

by

Thomas Molar

Molnar

FRANCISCAN HERALD PRESS
1434 WEST 51st STREET ● CHICAGO, 60609

WITHDRAWN
Todd Wehr Memorial Library
Viterbo College—La Crosse, WI

© 1978
Franciscan Herald Press
1434 West 51st Street Chicago, Illinois 60609

All Rights Reserved

Library of Congress Cataloging in Publication Data

Molnar, Thomas Steven.
  Christian humanism.

  1. Humanism, Religious. I. Title.
BL2747.6.M65   211'.6   78-2644
ISBN 0-8199-0694-8

NIHIL OBSTAT:
  Mark Hegener, O.F.M.
  Censor Deputatus

IMPRIMATUR:
  Msgr. Richard A. Rosemeyer, J.C.D.
  Vicar General, Archdiocese of Chicago

March 15, 1978

"The Nihil Obstat and the Imprimatur are official declarations that a book or pamphlet is free of doctrinal and moral error. No implication is contained therein that those who has granted the Nihil Obstat and Imprimatur agree with the contents, opinions or statements expressed."

MADE IN THE UNITED STATES OF AMERICA

BL 2747.6
.M65
1978

6.00

Herald Book Club

31 August '78

1017279

"To the memory of my Mother"

Foreword

An increasing number of Americans—in their capacity as parents, lawyers, teachers, judges—are worried today about the sudden appearance in schools, media, and legislatures of terms like humanism, secular humanism, humanistic religion, autonomous values, self-creation, situation ethics, secular city, sensitivity training, and so on. Upon a closer examination of textbooks, directives to teachers, curricula in schools of education, and tests administered to pupils and students, they find that the issue is not merely a temporary inroad by a fashionable fad, not even a mere ideology; all of us face a veritable religion whose terms and content may well be contrasted with the form and content of the Christian religion and the Hebrew-Christian tradition.

The humanistic religion has been detected in several areas of the country and is being fought—sporadically—by groups of parents, local newspapers, and here and there an isolated legislator, but the movement has many heads and even more ways of camouflaging itself under well-meaning labels with which it might be hard to quarrel. Even a pamphlet recently written against the humanistic creed begins its denunciation with a seemingly harmless definition: "A way of looking at the world which emphasizes the importance of man—his nature or his place in the universe." Then it goes on: "A humanist is one who believes that the welfare of the individual is more important than a strict interpretation of the laws." Now neither of these two sentences is entirely a correct statement about humanism; moreover, what they state describes nothing particularly evil. All philosophies begin with an inquiry into man's place in the universe, and the welfare of man may indeed have to take precedence at times over a strict interpretation of the law. There are similar cases of half-error, incompleteness, and superficialities in the rest of the brochure.

The consequence is that those who are determined to take up arms against the humanist creed are not always well prepared to do so. Often they argue that their children are easily misled by the psychosocially centered education, yet they forget that they themselves, whose education is supposed to have been guided by correct norms, are not much better off in this matter. First of all, they assume that the humanist religion is a kind of suddenly hatched conspiracy: by textbook publishers, professors of education, leftist ideologues—when truth is that ever since (at least) the Greek sophists, for example Protagoras, and up to sociologist Hans Kelsen who died a few years ago, humanism has had many representatives and it has been combatted by distinguished thinkers, from Plato to the present day. Thus, it may not be very effective in the long run to fight humanism in the public schools by taking the case (or the cases) to the courts and referring to the Constitution which forbids the teaching of religion in schools, thus the "humanist religion" too. The adepts of humanism may, indeed, boast at times that they constitute a "religion," but other adepts at other times may not make such claim at all. On the contrary, they may argue that their theories are scientific and that, as such, they enact a salubrious purgation of all religions. At any rate, one cannot counter an old and experienced worldview with lawsuits: One must meet its challenge in the arena of ideas, of knowledge of history and of philosophy. Quick lectures by no matter how justifiably irate parents or legal experts do not touch the core of the issue which will be revived again and again unless the whole cultural arsenal of educated men is systematically arrayed against it.

Let us add that the schools are not the only places involved in this controversy but also the religious debate in the lives of individuals, institutions, indeed of the church. For many centuries humanism was not taught in schools—at least not overtly—and education was in the hands of the clergy. Yet humanism as such grew and prospered outside the Catholic institutions, although it was opposed by Church, State, and the entire structure of Christian civilization. Thus, the issue transcends by far the one on which parents focus at present. Nor can the issue be "won" once and for all; it will revive regardless of the courts' decisions. It is then a religious and cultural obligation for all reasonable men to understand it in depth and, whenever possible, to use rational arguments *ad majorem Dei gloriam* against it.

In view of these considerations—the education of Christians in matters humanistic—this short book is divided into three parts:

Chapter One gives a historical and philosophical background of the origin and growth of man-centered—humanist—ideology in the West;

Chapter Two examines the issue whether a "Christian humanism" is a valid concept, and if so, within what limits. By necessity, this Chapter covers again some of the areas already discussed in the first Chapter, so as to illuminate them in a new, Christ-centered, light;

Chapter Three organizes the arguments against the radical innovators in the Church, after showing that their chief inspiration—under various labels—is radical humanism.

A book of this size cannot be expected to treat the problem of humanism exhaustively. It is hoped, however, that it presents the issue in the reflective framework it demands and deserves, and that it proves useful, less in the court cases of the near future—since the constitutional

issues are not discussed—than in the long-range debate
opposing Christians to a formidable antitheistic ideology.

Contents

CHAPTER

1.

The Humanist Ideology

For the first time since the Renaissance, the term *humanism* has again become fashionable during the last few decades. But long ago detached from its original, pre-Renaissance meaning—the discovery and comparative study of old manuscripts on which Greek and Roman works were copied by medieval scribes and clerks—the term has been mostly used, as in the various "Humanist Manifestoes," as an alternative to monotheistic religion, the expression of a man-centered worldview. Since quite recently, beginning with the Second Vatican Council, an increasing number of Catholic theologians, prelates and priests have taken up the term and made it current by introducing it into all sorts of documents, pastoral activities, and even catechetic manuals. One may thus speak of a veritable vogue of Humanism and humanists inside the Church, because the Church, with its tightly knit structure, is able to promote it through many channels. Yet the term, after centuries of sponsorship by materialist and anti-Christian thinkers, from Pomponazzi in the fifteenth to Bertrand Russell in the twentieth century, creates among Christians either a hostile reaction, or at least an uncomfortable feeling, based on confusion: What *is* humanism? Why its present vogue? Is it the opposite of Christian faith and doctrine? Is it compatible with them? Is there such a thing as a Christian Humanism? Is it part of orthodoxy? When Freemasons, relativists or ethical culturists, even Marxists, use the word in reference to themselves, does the usage conform with their long-held views, or does it indicate a rapprochement with traditional religions?

Such questions are signs of deep spiritual and intellectual trouble in which Christians often find themselves nowadays. It is compounded by the increasing confusion spread by the channels of our verbose civilization: myriad words pouring daily from the media, speeches, lectures, college courses, ad-hoc literature, advertisement—the targets of all this, the people, are unable to arrange these words in the correct boxes, thereby giving each word its appropriate place of importance or nonimportance. Those who propose their verbal ware use key words like humanism in combination with others, the consequence being that one would have to multiply indefinitely one's "boxes" so as to accommodate not just the terms themselves, but also the products of their cross-references with other terms.

For all these reasons, it might be advisable to explore humanism, its history, meaning, uses and implications, so as to present its roots and fruits, as well as to trace its significance for Christian thought and Christian life. It is thus hoped that the reader becomes better acquainted with a term likely to acquire an increasing importance as our public worldview—and jointly our social, political, and cultural attitudes—gradually detach themselves from traditional religious premises.

In a real and genuine sense Christianity is a human and humanized religion—but in order to grasp the essence of this statement we must set aside fashion and ideology, and gain a historical understanding of the issue. Born in the pagan civilization of the Hellenistic-Roman world, Christianity reacted to the prevailing views, systems, and assumptions, in other words, to the intellectual environment. Christian thinking was, naturally, not only a reaction to the milieu, it was primarily a new concept, a renovation of that milieu through a doctrine profoundly incompatible with pagan philosophy and science. The pagan worldview, and this is true of Greek, Iranian, Chaldean, Egyptian and Indian speculation, the total pre-Christian world picture, was based on the belief that the universe is peopled with gods and spirits, both benevolent and malevolent, that history is mechanically moving in a circular manner, always returning to the same point, and hence States and individuals are near-fatalistically tied to a pattern from which there is no escape. The Roman form of religion, moving between the *magic* which influences gods and spirits, and *pietas,* the performance of rites honoring the ancestors, stressed man's dependence on all sorts of forces which had to be constantly appeased and propitiated. The great contemporary historian of philosophy, Emil Bréhier, puts it clearly: "The cosmos of the Greeks was a world, so to speak, without history, a permanent order where time had practically no importance: it either preserved an unchanging order, or engendered a series of events returning always to the same point according to cyclical changes indefinitely repeated." The reverse concept, Bréhier continues, was introduced by the Christian worldview: that "there are in actuality radical changes and novelties was inconceivable before Christianity had not arrived to turn upside down the Greek cosmos."[1]

How did the Christian religion free the universe from its teeming gods, goddesses, and spirits, and introduce a concept of history which endowed man with a considerable freedom of action and responsibility? This was done, primarily, by monotheism, the belief in one single God who was not part of, but the external creator of, the universe, and who tolerated "no other gods" in his exclusive worship. With the creation of Adam, this God entered in a dialogue with man, placing him under his providence, yet allowing him enough freedom to become a *person,* a steward of nature and a keeper of his brother. Henceforth, history was not an eternally-the-same cycle, it was more like a straight line with a sequence of novelties produced by the incalculable interplay of men among themselves and of God and mankind. St. Augustine was among the first to formulate this idea, saying that history takes it course along a line "from creation to last judgment. . . . Every particular event, every human life and action, is a unique phenomenon under providence and must have a definite meaning."[2] In St. Augustine's mind, this "line" was not a progression in the modern sense of improvement; rather, his commentator adds, "it was the *operatio Dei* in time, a one-directional, teleological process, directed to one goal—the salvation of individual men, not of any collective groups."[3]

But there was more to the rehabilitation of man than his personhood and dialogue with the living God. While these elements were present already in the Old Testament, Jesus Christ brought a new element to the historical drama: his incarnation, his being man and God. In one divine *person,* the Catholic religion teaches, Jesus has two *natures (totus deus et totus homo);* his human nature is ontologically structured as that of man, but it is perfected by its connection with divine nature. Hence it is not corrupted like man's nature, it is not engaged in any vice, it does not indulge in, or commit, sin.[4]

The "humanization" implemented by Christianity through Christ's two natures was regarded with consternation by the pagan intellectuals. It is important to stop for a moment on this issue since so many false ideas about it have been made current in two thousand years of history. The critics of the Church tried to prove that Christianity favors an otherworldly, abstract, belittling view of man, over against the healthy, concrete, and natural view propagated by pagan sages, priests and statesmen. Even Arius the heresiarch is enlisted by these critics as a "humanist"; truth is, this disciple of Plotinus denied the divine/human consubstantiality of Christ not because he was an enlightened humanist, but because in the abstract Plotinian view which he shared, there is at the origin an impersonal "One" from which the rest of the world proceeds by emanations (hypostases): In the Arian system Jesus Christ was the first of these emanations, a theory welcomed by pagan intellectuals and by Christians seeking a compromise with the intellectual fashion. It is obvious, however, that the Plotinian/Arian theory does not conceive of Christ as a human being since in the master's system man occupies a rather low rank among the emanations. (Much later, the thinkers of the Enlightenment who launched the modern attack against Christianity were also to argue that it is an antihuman system pursuing an ascetic ideal and repressing the normal human instincts. Hegel and his generation of idealists saw in the Greek gods of Olympus full-blooded projections of the Greek ideal of a life of this-worldly pleasures; they did not care to register the fact that the greatest of Hellas's philosophers had rejected the all-too earthly conception of the Olympian/Homeric gods as unworthy of representing the morally dimensioned human beings). The most prominent ancient critic of Christianity, the Roman Celsus (170 A.D.) also rejected with undisguised horror the idea of an incarnate God who wants to be so near to the human concern as to assume human nature. Why should God come down from his carefree existence, asked Celsus; why would he wish to turn the universe upside down? Does he not know that the slightest change in the eternal immutability would start the general collapse of the whole? If indeed he comes among men, he subjects himself to change, for all change is a diminution.[5]

What Celsus and the other Greek and Roman critics of Christianity found also inacceptable—and this shows, contrary to Hegel's assumption, their antihuman stance—is that the Christian God did not merely volunteer to become man, he chose to be born from a most humble status, a Galilean cabinetmaker, led an existence among socially humble people, outcasts, and accepted the ignominious death reserved for slaves and criminals. For the esthetically refined pagan intellectuals, belief in such a man was more than a scandal and a folly, it showed an inferior and perverse turn of mind, fully justifying the persecution and extermination of its adepts. In other words, pagan thought remained obstinately unresponsive to the true "humanism" that Christianity taught, and continued insisting on the complete separation of the happy gods living a life of uncaring pleasure and man burdened by misery and suffering. Yet, when a thousand years later the Renaissance reacquainted itself with ancient thought in its length and width, it regarded that thought as humane and humanistic, relegating Christianity to the category of obscurantism and superstition. Increasingly, from the Renaissance to the nineteenth century, modern humanist spokesmen took up the old Roman slogan according to which "Christians hated the human race," when in fact later Roman critics had grudgingly admitted—and recommended for imitation—the charity and mutual care demonstrated by the early Christians. "From the time of Marcus Aurelius [a contemporary of Celsus] paganism makes increasing attempts to reform itself on the model of the religion which threatens its existence and with which it is at war."[6] This imitation and self-reformation consisted of a growing tendency to resolve polytheism in favor of one God, to regard this God as the source of moral commandments, and to teach the worshiper to imitate the good God in his daily dealings.

There is no reason for believers of the Christian religion to blush when they hear the charges of ancient, Renaissance, or contemporary humanists. While any word ending in *ism* may be regarded as at least suspect of an ideology, it is best to call Christianity a *humane* religion, on the ground of the previous arguments. Without discussing now what Christianity represents in the area of faith and religious thought, let us state that on all other levels too it represented a great and decisive improvement over paganism:
    a) by clearing the universe of its many gods, spirits and occult forces, Christianity not only purified the concept of the divinity, it also prepared the way for *science*. The scientific enterprise became unencumbered by the myriad imaginary entities which had peopled nature and heaven, so that exploration and speculation were able to begin about celestial mechanics and the other workings of nature;
    b) by sponsoring a view of history no longer conceived as a prison in which the individual and his community were chained to the inexorable turning of gigantic wheels, the cycles of time, Christianity created *history* as neither a simple chronicle of events (which it was still with Herodo-

tus), nor a pessimistic outlook forecasting the ultimate decline of all time-bound formations, thus their essential meaninglessness (the view of Polybius);

c) by making man an ethical being, endowed with dignity by God, creator of his soul and merciful for his sins, Christianity laid down the preconditions of meaningful *political and social* action in the framework of institutions that are incomparable with any other: institutions based on spiritual as well as temporal loyalty, not in contradiction but in freedom-creating tension.

Against these rather considerable credentials, Humanism nevertheless claims that the Christian religion has restricted man's scope, narrowed his horizon, and thwarted his efforts at individual and collective improvement. The representatives of Humanism always considered it as their role and mission to remedy this situation, in either of two ways:

a) work for the enlightenment of man plunged since the founding of Christianity into obscurantism. This has been the objective of such humanistic movements as Freemasonry, the positivistic philosophy of Auguste Comte, radical humanism, etc.;

b) persuade Christians, more especially the Church of Rome, to humanize their religion through concessions to the humanistic ideal, and meanwhile to synchronize the worldly (political, social) actions of groups of Christians and humanists.[7]

Facing these arguments and this strategy, we must discuss in the following such problems as human nature and freedom, and their relationship with the Christian teaching. Contemporary humanists, as we shall see later, put forward some rather simplistic arguments about the narrowness and antihuman attitude of the Christian worldview. This is all the more surprising as earlier humanistic thought, still nourished by its organic contact with Christian philosophy, arrayed far more cogent arguments and displayed a depth not usually found today in humanistic literature. As we shall also see later, there are reasons for the progressive poverty and primitiveness of the humanist arsenal, emptied of its faith in proportion to it becoming fashionable as a creed, a way of thinking, and a style of life.

If in its encounter and clash with pagan speculation[8] Christianity accomplished the intellectual and spiritual liberation of the universe and of men, it never taught that there were no limits to this freedom. First, there is the limit of revelation. We quote again St. Augustine who gave the Church, and indeed the post-Roman western world, not only their first great philosophy of history, but also the richly argued thesis that God revealed to Moses and to Christ all truth to be communicated to man and history, and that henceforth there is no new lesson to teach. No progress is to be found in the course of human history, in spite of coming stupendous inventions and discoveries. "Two things run the course together, the evil derived from Adam and the good bestowed by the creator."[9] Such an all-encompassing view is bound to provoke, if not outright disagreement, at least further nuanced argument in the mind of those shocked by its clearly stated definitiveness. Not yet the humanists, since they did not appear on the scene before the late fourteenth century, but thinkers inside the Church who quite often collided with St. Augustine and his heritage on this issue.

The plain teaching of the Church—in reality of all monotheistic religions—is that God being perfection, his creations are less than perfect, although *qua* creatures, thus enjoying the divine sollicitude and love, they are good, that is perfect, in themselves. "Perfect" and "good" mean here something like "finished product" with a potential for growth, enrichment, and betterment, but not going beyond a certain, rather clearly observable, limit. As the philosopher Leo Strauss puts it, man is free, yet he also has a nature; while we cannot predict the new things that he might do—for good as well as for evil—we know within what limits they will occur.[10] We know it by introspection since every soul is a mirror of the other souls, by personal experience, and by the vicarious experience of history, literature, art, medicine, etc.

Particularly in the latter half of the Middle Ages, the controversy developed as part of a larger debate concerning the perfectibility of man. Such a term was, of course, not used before the eighteenth century; the medieval version of the issue was expressed in a different way, suggesting, with all the circumspection of scholarship and relying partly on the Gospel of St. John, that man has within his power to become in some sense divine. At all times there were people who took their own fervor and enthusiasm for the expression of an inner voice, God's personal communication to them, which they were called to reveal to an intimate circle of select believers or to the whole world. The Greeks had known such people as *mystes,* the Romans as *vates,* the Hebrews as *prophets,* the Christians as *mystics.* At all times also a great deal of attention was paid to the problem how to distinguish the true from the false prophet; the only way that seemed reasonable was to verify whether the person in question was merely and in the long run a self-seeking fellow, a fanatic ready to commit violence, or one whose life was accorded to his words, who lived a good and moral existence, devoted himself to the service of others, and acted within the sacramental and doctrinal tradition of his religion. There are, naturally, borderline cases so that each case requires careful observation and investigation. Msgr. Ronald Knox in his book on *Enthusiasm,* Norman Cohn in *The Pursuit of the Millenium,* Walter Nigg in *The Heretics,* Thomas Molnar in *Utopia, the Perennial Heresy,* and many others have elaborated criteria by which the words and deeds of men of God may be evaluated. St. John of the Cross prescribed, for example, that every Christian ought to work on the nurture of his soul under the supervision of his director so that an objective outsider might check his self-glorying enthusiasm as he deepens in himself the search for God. The medieval Flemish mystic, Ruysbroeck, taught that while it is true that in the course of spiritual enrichment the ordinary human values must be transcended, they ought not to be abandoned. Even in the moment of mystical union with God, these values are present. Indeed, the practice of the mystic himself, writes Ruysbroeck, consists of turning toward God and of returning to the world.[11] This does not mean to be a divided man, a confused soul, it means precisely the orthodox solution for which the human being was created: the adoration of God demands, as a natural effect, the sharing of the spiritual treasure with other men.

Ruysbroeck was not alone in the fourteenth century to teach true mysticism, thus the true evaluation of the mystic's —and to a lesser degree, of all men's — task, distant from excessive enthusiasm which ends in self-divinization. From the eleventh century on and into the fifteenth, there were several regions in Europe where some form of "enthusiasm" (Knox calls it also "ultra-supernaturalism") had developed, rapidly degenerating into heresy or, at least, into strange philosophical systems, exaggerated practices, and mass-movements reminiscent of those we may observe these days among "flower children," "hippies" and "commune" dwellers. Such areas of concentrated practice were the Rhine Valley, the South of France, Calabria, the North of Italy, the Balkans, and proof exists of the contacts established among these groups along waterways and the roads traveled by merchants, soldiers, pilgrims, and vagabonds. The pattern of these sects, movements, and cultic associations was the following: Gathered around a preacher, people would be initiated in the "secret core of doctrine" which, in manifest disagreement with the Church's magisterium, would overemphasize certain aspects of dogma or credo, sacraments or works. Usually, the movement's set of beliefs was that man or at least a select few, had been turned into purely spiritual beings by the Gospels, and need no sacraments nor works (morality) since they possess in themselves the plenitude of intellect and of the Holy Spirit. As a consequence, they and their adepts regard themselves as authorized to reject the Church's teaching and practices, indeed to consider the Church as a corrupt deviation from Christ's words and themselves as the true Church. The conviction that the spirit was acting in them led these members often to an immoral way of life, a communism of goods and women, and violence against those who disagreed.

The origin of these movements, the Brothers of the Free Spirit, the Amaurians, the Cathars, the Bogomils, the Fraticelli, the Beghards, and numerous others, can be found in most cases in the gnostic, Manichaean, and other sects that had flourished a thousand years before, but were compelled by the Church to disband or go "underground." They surfaced again in Western Europe when communal life was restored in towns and pilgrimages, after the fearful centuries of barbarian invasions which ended only in the tenth century. But what is here described in a sketchy form is meant only to serve as a background for three outstanding personalities: mystics and philosophers, whose ideas contributed, although at first indirectly, to the formulation of humanistic ideology.

In spite of the short space at our disposal, we must be careful in our evaluation of these men. It is not a question of suspecting them of lack of orthodox beliefs; in fact they may be greeted as illustrations of the freedom of thought that the Church has tolerated within the limits that every human community recognizes as the law of persisting in its being and identity. Yet, by certain aspects of their thought, these men, progressively from the first to the last discussed, prepared the thinking of others who then went far beyond the permissible limits.[12]

Chronologically, the first of these men was Joachim, abbot of Fiore, in Southern Italy (twelfth century). From the point of view of today's Humanism, he would have to be called a typical "medieval man," a mystic concerned with the increased spiritualization of the Church, not with the full development of human potentialities in the mundane order. Yet, Joachim came to two important conclusions, easily "humanized" by later thought:

a) it is possible for man to understand the structure of history and predict its course;[13]

b) the revelation taught by the Church was not the last one, after the Age of the Old Testament and that of the New Testament there will be a Third Age, that of the Holy Spirit.[14]

It is not clear in the eyes of scholars whether Joachim himself or his followers after his death in 1204 propagated the notion that the Third Age would be sponsored by a Third Gospel (called also "Eternal"), and that the year of the great changeover was to be 1260. Anyway, when the appointed year passed without such novelties, Joachim's disciples fixed a new date, 1290, with no more success. But if certain details cannot yet be established with certainty, there is no doubt about Joachim's teaching. His premises were that in the Third Age the new, spiritual man would know the truth without veil and receive directly from the Holy Spirit all the charismatic gifts necessary for perfection. Implied in this was the abolition, in that final period, of the Church as an institution for the guidance of the soul, of sacraments as channels of grace, and of the clergy as mediators—although the Third Age was to be guided by "the monks" of whom one assumes that they would have been an order of the "elect."

Joachim's preaching fomented an atmosphere of crisis and of expectations of a new revelation. As in the case of later prophets of the "enthusiastic" kind, his visions of the imminent future provoked widespread exaltation, and had a direct impact on the so-called "spiritual" Franciscans who combined the Joachitic pattern of history with the life and teaching of their own master, St. Francis. It was tempting for them to interpret the foundation of their Order as the beginning of the Third Age and the figure of Francis as the new Jesus Christ, in fact superior to Jesus Christ because he accepted and imposed absolute poverty whereas Jesus and the Apostles did handle money and did have modest belongings.

Joachim's stature, teaching, and influence are, then, not to be compared with those of Francis who accepted his insertion in the Church and in history. Joachim, on the other hand, was quite a "modern" figure insofar as he re-interpreted history, dividing it according to the tripartite scheme, later popularized by such outstanding thinkers of modernity as Condorcet, Hegel, Comte and Marx. In Joachim's apocalyptic interpretation the three ages were the Age of Law (Father), the Age of Grace (Son), and the Age of Love (Holy Spirit). In other words, the Calabrian Abbot saw in history a similar kind of maturation process as many of our contemporary intellectuals, among them Fr. Teilhard de Chardin and the humanists. It is quite significant, for example, that Joachim appraised the "second age," that of Christ, as a preparatory one and referred to it merely as situated "between the two others" (*inter utrumque*), a trans-itional period with faults and deficiencies to be soon cor-rected. In other words, he did not announce an apocalyptic end of history, followed by the last judgment, but, like many ideologues later, a new world order where men would cease being *viatores* and become *comprehensores*, distin-guished in medieval terminology between the travelers toward salvation and those who have arrived at Truth.

Joachim is thus the first major systematizer of the ideology of this-worldly perfection, and the fact that he gave the notion of the apocalypse a new and revolutionary inter-pretation (for which he was greatly admired) only shows the depth of this revolution: A transhistorical concept was for the first time pressed in the service of mundane events, of history. The immediate and logical upshot of this eschato-logical movement was to challenge the Church by pointing at the discrepancy between absolute spiritual purity repre-sented by the movement or sect and the imperfections, de-fects, and worldly concessions maculating the institutional Church. The controversy was not quite new to Joachim's time; as a favorite topic of New Testament criticism it goes back to the first century. Scholars since the eighteenth century have been asserting that Jesus had no intention of founding a "Church"; the formula: "Tu es Petrus . . ." would be a later interpolation for the Church's self–justification. Jesus and his immediate followers expected the rapid fulfillment of prophecies concerning the end of the world. When this did not happen, the argument runs, an institution was established as a kind of unavoidable compromise. Indeed, it is quite probable that there were in the first century around and after Jesus, as also in Joachim's time, groups of enthusiasts expecting the end of the world and the opening of Heaven *hic et nunc;* there are in every epoch impatient people demanding eschaton now—just as the hippies demanded Paradise Now! a few years ago. These impatient people would agree with the Italian scholar, E. Buonaiuti, who has made himself a spokesman for the "spiritual Church." He writes: "The idea that a long interval must precede the coming of the kingdom, and that this interval requires the foundation of a visible, hierarchically ordered church, is utterly alien to Christ's central thought." Buonaiuti interprets the history of conflicts between the Church and the heretical sects as "atempts [on the part of the sects] to defend the ecclesia spiritualis against the forces of profanation which menaced its innermost being."[15]

It is not hard to evaluate the import of this conflict. By remaining obstinately distant, the false eschaton causes its adepts to lose patience; while they continue accusing the Church of not yielding to their demand of instant spiritualization, they turn to immediately available secular, thus seemingly more efficacious, doctrines to satisfy their thirst for perfection; in their fervid imagination they endow the secular doctrines (ideologies) with the spiritual dimension that the Church is supposed to have lost. The "enthusiasts" then slip more and more easily away from the Church's doctrinal and sacramental life, into an ideological partisanship; after a while the highly upheld spirituality, no longer supported by the now despised ecclesiastical structure, turns into a purely mundane militancy for revolutionary causes, and the Kingdom of God is exchanged for the Secular City as the ultimate objective.[16] Here then is at least one of the roots of Humanism although it is camouflaged from our eyes by the intense spirituality of a doctrine like Joachim's whose manifest goal is to rise above the human problematics. In this light, the warnings of Ruysbroeck, Jacopo de Todi, St. John of the Cross, and other mystics becomes transparently clear: the true spiritual man proves that he belongs to God by holding on to both anchors of his existence, the divine and the human, in an exact imitation of the incarnate Jesus Christ. The human in him is, of course, illumined and transfixed by the divine; but he never takes this as a sign of the transmutation of his human essence into divine essence, he remains contented and free within his *status creaturae*. It is not a desire of self–promotion to divinity which informs his actions, he derives from his commerce with God a more thoroughly lived charity and love turned to the spiritual and physical advantage of his fellow creatures. Compare, in this respect, St. Francis and those of his followers, the so-called "spiritual" Franciscans, who wanted to place him above Christ, regarded themselves as new men, and turned to Joachim in quest of a more valid, "eternal gospel." Francis never thought of claiming an extraordinary status either for himself or for the Order he founded, he was poor in spirit, not because he refused pedantically to own a piece of clothing, but because he trod in the Lord's footsteps and had no thought of refusing obedience to Pope and Church. Another saint, Bernard, also showed in both word and example that true spirituality does not imply giving up the human status and the need for men to live in organized communities even when salvation is the aim, particularly when salvation is the aim. This is what St. Bernard wrote to the new bishop of Cologne: "Remain at your post, make all the efforts to be useful to those you govern, and do not try to escape the duty to command as long as you do it in view of their good. Beware of putting your authority to wrong use; but beware even more of avoiding to be useful for fear of commanding."[17]

We sought in the Joachitic deviation from orthodoxy not the actual origin of Humanism, only one important root of its substance: the exaltation of man who insists, although in the name of more spirituality, on breaking down his creaturely status. Thus, from an apparent modesty and deepened inner life—the rejection of externals like sacraments, hierarchy, institution—the humanist and even the prehumanist took the leap toward absolute pride as if to be simply human were a cause for shame.

In the philosophy of Nicholas of Cusa we shall seek the subtle dissolution of the concept of God as a person and the consequent rise of man to a higher status in what may be called a quasipantheistic system of thought. It should be understood that the two centuries between Joachim (died in 1204) and Nicholas (born in 1401) were not a vacuum from the point of view which interests us here, the exploration of Humanism's early roots; the chain of ideas leading from the one to the other was uninterrupted. If we omit the discussion of the interval, it is for reasons of space and in order not to break the unity of the argument.

Like Joachim, Nicholas was an ecclesiastic, and like the Abbot, he was never officially criticised for his similarly daring, unorthodox views, in fact, he was made a bishop quite young, then was elevated to the cardinalate by his friend, the humanist Aeneas Sylvius, known as Pope Pius II. Nicholas advised the pope on many issues, most importantly on the healing of the schism with the Eastern Church. The bishop was already a Renaissance figure, as was also the pope, a traveler, a great reader and collector of Greek and Latin manuscripts, a serious scientist deeply involved in the study of mathematics, geometry and astronomy. On the other hand, and this only underlines the Renaissance-type versatility, his speculation was heir to "a long apophatic tradition[18] with such men influencing him as Plotinus,

Pseudo-Denys, the Rhine-valley mystics, Meister Eckhart and Johannes Tauler,"[19]

We must now attempt to systematize the thought of Cusanus, a difficult task since he drew from many sources and made himself the confluence of numerous intellectual trends. We might suggest that this extremely subtle mind had a two-tiered project, although without necessarily being aware of it, as genuine and original thinkers produce in one jet, and often only their commentators see how the thought is structured. Let us then say that the system of Nicholas can be divided into

a) a quasipantheistic conception of the universe of which God is not an external creator, but rather a principle of growth and a limit of potentialities; and

b) the universe itself which is not furnished with given models or objects, but is a network of relationships, participations, and interpenetrations, and even more audaciously conceived, a progressive construction of the human intelligence.

For Nicholas to elaborate such a philosophy, he had to contradict the Church's position on a number of points, and had to manipulate it beyond recognition at other points. Support in his work was provided by the imminent discreditation of the Aristotelian system of science. The Stagirite's image of the cosmos: the supralunar world of eternally ordained movements and the sublunar world of imperfectly imitating motions—began to collapse, not because of the rise of experimental science (this was still a century and a half away), but on account of new mathematical calculations. But even for mathematical calculations to become accepted, a bold view of the totality was needed, and this Cusanus supplied. Concerning harmony in the cosmos, he suggested, it is irrelevant to ask whether this is indeed the case, it is better to assume our ignorance of it and postulate that the human mind introduces order into the motions of things as it observes them. This was a revolutionary step, one on which modern science was to rest for centuries; we may call it "knowledge by unknowing," we are entitled to do so by Nicholas himself who called his speculative system by the global term of "knowing ignorance" (*docta ignorantia*). To him it seemed as if man, unable to penetrate the nature of things with his senses, must rely on his mind (*mens*) to construct a manageable view of things. The principle of this construction, and this is the crucial point, has, in a way, nothing to do with God who, Nicholas held, should not be understood as a potter making a vase, that is an extrinsic creator, but as something endowing things with essence and comprehending them at the same time. God is thus an intracosmic force, not creating ex nihilo, and conceivable only as the infinity immanent in finite things, being the limit of their virtualities. In M. de Gandillac's characterization, the center of Cusanus' philosophy is the divine/human intellect as it tries to capture the phenomena, themselves indefinite, in an ever-renewed system of indeterminate units.[20] All one knows is that in the permanent flux of phenomena and their uncertain grasp by a self-making mind, the only "fix" point—it measures nothing, it is a mere description—is the conpenetration of phenomena and qualities (*coincidentia oppositorum*) due to the participation of each of them in the totality.

Thus, although Cusanus's speculation is shot through with uncertainty, relativism, and approximation, and therefore represents a major break with the Aristotelian world of substances, forms, and concepts and opens on modern scientific thought—it has very definite consequences for the Christian religion. The general method of approximations may have released scientific imagination from Aristotle's conceptual edifice and thus fecundated it for future discoveries; but it is obvious that the God who says "I am who I am" is not a usable concept for Cusanus. God, also called by him "Not-Other" (*non-aliud*) becomes a kind of guarantee that in the infinite all the contraries will meet and coincide: the curve and the straight line, the cold and the hot, the word and silence, soul and divinity. Thus, following the Rhineland mystics, Cusanus suggests that the soul contains God, that grace too is dormant in it (J. Tauler's point), that nothing may be stated of God without its opposite being stated also. Objective statements about God and religion are disqualified, the human being obtains all that God is compelled to shed in the process. In an early work, Nicholas had stated that faith alone saves and that the sacraments are only "signs"[21]; as a cardinal, he later concluded that the words of the Apostolic Creed, Father, Son, and Holy Spirit, are "imprecise" and recommended a better approximation through logic and psychology.

"God" (in quotation marks because he becomes more a force than a personal creator) is thus made to find his place in an ingeniously constructed system with serious ambitions to be scientific in the modern sense. In the process of elaborating the system, the Christian religion, insofar as it is regarded as important at all in comparison with the "worldview" to which it is made to yield, becomes an adjunct to a philosophical system, something against which thinkers like Pascal and Gilson were to object in the Cartesian system. It is quite evident that, like Descartes, Cusanus did not need God for the formulation of his science; he introduced "God" because, again like Descartes, he was a Christian, and in all likelihood, a sincere believer. Yet, later thinkers, religiously more indifferent than Cusanus, were to drop the facade and work on their philosophies with man at its center, which is not quite the case yet for Nicholas. For a while, "God" remained either as the giver of the initial impetus to the system, as with Descartes, or as an explanatory device of the ultimate equation, the case of Cusanus. But whether God is pressed into service at the beginning or at the end, speculation launched on these rails must put man in the dizzying position of an absolute—with Cusanus it is the paradoxical position of a relative absolute—as a "second God," the copula of all things, the spirit whose mission is to lead the cosmos to its final end. It was no coincidence that radical Humanism took shape in the century that began with Nicholas's birth and saw, toward its closing years, the death of Pico della Mirandola.

The latter, an Italian nobleman of such an extraordinary knowledge that his contemporaries saw in him the world's miracle, was two generations closer than Nicholas to the essence of Renaissance spirit. He was also nearer the humanist type than the Cardinal, in fact the now fully developing humanist trends find a meeting place in his versatile and restless mind. Before turning our attention to him, it will be advisable to outline the humanist movement and understand the varied, yet ultimately unified meaning one must assign to the term.

"Human" as contrasted with "divine" disciplines were those, beginning with the fourteenth century, which dealt not with Hebrew and Christian literature about God, the sacred writings and their commentaries, but with pagan literature from Greece and Rome. The term thus meant originally something like literature *not* dealing with scripture, theology, apologetics, and the documents of doctors and councils. By the nature of things, the manuscripts of humanist literature had been more difficult to find and the correctness of their surviving copies studied, than those of divine literature, carefully collated and organized by ecclesiastical authorities and scholars. The humanists were those—both ecclesiastics and laymen—whose interest in ancient literature: Cicero, Virgil, Horace, Seneca, Plutarch, Pliny, etc., led them to locate the manuscripts, compare them for authenticity, establish the most reliable version, and study their language and style. This endeavor was nothing less than a full-scale science, that of philology, comparative linguistics, literature, analysis of data, and other disciplines. In principle, this science had no scope contrary to that of the divine sciences, and there was no intrinsic reason why the two should collide. However, by the fifteenth century signs of collision emerged and multiplied. The humanist Lorenzo Valla established, for example, that the alleged document called the "donation of Constantine," on which the papacy had based for a thousand years its right to the papal State, was a post-Constantine forgery. If such was the case, other Church and religious writings could also be challenged. Yet, this was not the substance of the issue. Increasingly, Humanism came to mean not only the critical scrutiny of documents, sacred and profane, but also an independent stance vis-a-vis Christian doctrine. By the late fifteenth and early sixteenth century those whom we call humanists were often students of the University of Padua where, among other things, the philosophy of Averroes was taught and admired, in contradiction to that of Aristotle that St. Thomas had found as the most compatible system of thought with Christian doctrine. And Averroism's most popular proposition was the so-called thesis of the "two truths": *faith* is true in its own domain, and *reason* in its own; if the two do not clash, the Averroists taught, it is because faith is not reasonable, its articles cannot be demonstrated. Only what is demonstrable is of interest to reason, and that is the object of science: natural science, or magic and the occult sciences.[22] Matters of faith were consequently isolated from rational discourse, left in a compartment of their own, a compartment destined to fall into dust without the vitalizing interest of scientific exploration.

With these developments, it is easy to see that the term "Humanism" had lost its original meaning by about the year 1500. Many humanists, Thomas More, Erasmus, Melanchton, Reuchlin, Lefèvre d'Estaples, born in the previous century and of the same age as Pico or younger, got involved in the Catholic-Lutheran conflict and in national-political controversies; others, like Agrippa of Nettesheim and Paracelsus, turned to secret doctrines and magical manipulations; yet others, Pomponazzi and Etienne Dolet, almost openly advocated a return to pagan materialism, and were atheists. One might say with hardly any forcing of the comparison that the humanists of the fifteenth and sixteenth centuries were already similar to the intellectuals of the nineteenth and twentieth centuries: Both categories strike the student by the multiplicity of their interests and preoccupations; it is hard to find among them truly original minds; in the course of several generations their intellectual loyalty shifts from (religiously) orthodox to critical, then to radical and hostile.

Does Pico's figure correspond to this composite picture? Without any doubt, to parts of it. From his life and that of Cusanus, from their respective ambitions and achievements, one could in fact construct the ideal type of the humanist: not yet radical, utopian, bitter, excessive, and agnostic (or atheist) as many of their type were to be in the sixteenth century and later—but no longer orthodox either as their predecessors in the fourteenth, for example, the "prince of humanists" and poet laureate, Petrarch. They stand between these two types in the line of humanism's evolution, but marked already by an ideological bias in favor of man's autonomy. Etienne Gilson expressed surprise, for example, that the obvious utopianism of Cardinal Cusa was never censored by the Church; we may be equally surprised that Pico's concept of potentially divine man did not raise more eyebrows; true, he died so early that his full measure could not yet be taken.

The central idea of Nicholas and Pico, but more fully developed by the second while, although not for fear of censorship, it was still wrapped in mystery by Nicholas, was the potentiality of man to become indefinitely more than what the scriptural view had of him, in fact a "second God," not only grasping the universal meaning, also constructing the universe. Some modern scholars attribute this excessively sanguine image of man's potentialities to the enthusiastic expectations of the "first modern men" as they were stepping out of the "dark ages" and crossing the threshold to the Renaissance. Facts dictate a different view. As we have noted, the idea of the human being's limitless potentialities was not an echo of pagan thought, but a heritage of the Rhineland mystics and other so-called negative theologians (*theologia negativa*) who, like Meister Eckhart, for example, saw in man a sharer of God's soul, one element of the divine dyad, whom God needs as much as man needs God. The forceful personality and eloquent preaching of Eckhart brought him many and outstanding disciples, great mystics in their own right (Tauler, Suso, Thomas à Kempis), and even Cusanus himself, a mystic among philosophers or a philosopher among mystics, whichever way we wish to regard him. To the Rhinish school's influence another influence was added not later than the century of Nicholas and Pico: the Hermetic writings, attributed to the legendary Hermes Trismegistus whom both men, and their contemporaries, still believed to have been a great Egyptian sage in the days before Moses, endowed with a truly divine wisdom and insight in the secrets of the universe.[23] One can thus see that neither Nicholas nor Pico was an "enlightened" mind in the sense we use that term, that is in its eighteenth-century formulation. There is no question then of a Renaissance "enthusiasm" inspiring Nicholas and Pico and making them break some imaginary mental shackles.

The ambition to see man more than man is as old as humanity, although whether the ambition is acceptable to Christian minds depends on what the proponent means by it. We saw what Nicholas meant by it: Man, the "second God," was for him a co-creator of the universe together with God, both grasping the new things as they come into existence, less by creation than by a kind of spontaneous mental generation. Man was also the "copula," the link, of all phenomena which *become* in proportion as he grasps/invents their reality, quantity, quality, and other attributes.[24] Pico's imagination and ambition were fired perhaps more intensely than that of the Cardinal. The latter, a true oecumenic spirit and still very much a Christian, saw the use to which his speculation may be put on the practical plane, not as the exaltation of man but as his rise above the level of discord and conflict in matters of faith. The true vision of the universe which Nicholas thought he was demonstrating ought to help the adepts of all religions to agree on a commonly shared cult, a universal religion. In his *De pace fidei* he imagined an assembly of the representatives of all mankind obtaining from God the permission to set up the common cult in Jerusalem, then to appoint "administrative spirits" teaching (imposing?) it in all regions of the planet. [25]

The idea that Pico derived from the notion of man's "multiform potentiality," which, as we saw, was a line of current thinking among many, although by no means all, Christian scholars of the Renaissance, led him in other directions. It was not the first nor the last time that a brilliant intellect, taking his own versatility for a potential transcendence of the human condition by him, followed by all men, showed himself ignorant of the fact that even with vast erudition human beings remain morally limited. At any rate, Pico's central conviction seems to have been that all traditions: Hebrew, Egyptian, Greek, Arab, Cabalistic, Hermetic, etc., had beliefs similar to those held by Christians, and thus did not contradict, but rather supported, the truth of Christianity. The idioms in which they expressed the basically common insights were varied, but the essence was nearly identical. Pico's enormous reading and erudition persuaded him that he could successfully demonstrate this unity of religious and philosophical truth in nine hundred theses to be defended in Rome before an assembly of pope, prelates and scholars. His last years were spent on the elaboration of these theses in which all human knowledge would be lined up to impress the audience of the truth of their shared religion—and of a few other things beside. Since he never had a chance to defend his theses—some of its points were criticised and the Curia was reluctant to listen— it is best to turn to their introduction, Pico's *Oration on the Dignity of Man*.

The question at once arises whether what Pico intended to defend was really the Christian truth or a humanist truth?

The line of argument of the *Oration* is that man is privileged among creatures: the latter possess a determinate nature within which they exist and move; man is a pure indeterminacy, who is allowed by God to "trace the lineaments of his own nature." This, taken to its logical conclusion, would indeed make of man a second God. But there is more: God says to man that he was made "neither mortal nor immortal," a "fashioner of his own being." Further on, Pico calls upon his hearers, bishops and theologians, to lift themselves "to such ecstasy that our intellects and our very selves are united to God. . . . Borne outside ourselves, filled with the Godhead, we shall be no longer ourselves, but the very One who made us." The many pagan references: to Socratic frenzy, to the sacred name of Apollo, etc., might give the Oration the kind of Renaissance style of hyperbole found in the literature of the time and not necessarily binding the authors to a pagan worldview. However, Pico, the formidably erudite scholar, knew well that in the above quoted passages he went far beyond the Christian discourse. What is the creator God if his role vis-a-vis one particular creature, man, is limited to a kind of first shaping, after which man's real creator will be man himself? It is impossible to accept the view of Fr. Henri de Lubac, for example, who sees in Pico—and also in Cusanus—one who breaks through the timidity of certain Christians by proclaiming man as an unfinished being with unlimited self-effecting potentialities.[26] De Lubac quotes St. Augustine who wrote that "God is nearer to me than I am to myself," also a bold statement supposedly similar to Pico's "we shall be no longer ourselves, but the very One who made us." No such similarity exists: Augustine's saying could have come out of a child's mouth, referring to his father's greater care and foresight for him than his own for himself; Pico, on the other hand, deifies the creature through the typical process of a falsely mystical enthusiasm or frenzy, the kind that abounds in the writings of false mystics. This is how G. Gusdorf appraises Pico's position in the history of ideas: "There was in the Middle Ages a doctrine of freedom whose major preoccupation was to derive an explanation of human destiny from the word of God. This aspiration yielded to such conceptions which made of the individual the focus of all truth, in a world of which he is the master. . . . The values have their residence here below, the world depends on man. The process of making God yield his power to man was to take a few centuries, but already in the Renaissance one can see the first features of man whom Nietzsche will define as the great evaluator, the center and creator of values."[27]

Pico's death (1494)—and he was still a religious man, like Cusanus—symbolically announced that henceforth the struggle was on between the deocentric and the humanist (humano-centric) worldviews: both God and man could not be infinite, not even in Cusanus's conciliatory and subtle proposition that "the Infinite is immanent in the finite." Either God is infinite perfection—and then man is limited within his rich yet finite nature—or man has divine potentialities, in which case the notion of God's omnipotence—and essence—is at least blurred. Indeed, if the obligatory references to Christianity are removed from later humanist discourse, this is the impression left: a God increasingly marginal and abstract, and man, in that same proportion, acquiring the abandoned divine attributes. The result was similar—since the roots were the same—to what followed from contemporary (sixteenth-century) Protestant affirmation, as Louis Bouyer puts it: "The final consequence was to lock up God in an impossibility to communicate himself to man, and man unable to be torn from his own solitude, from the autonomy of his arrogant humility."[28]

At this point it may seem to the reader that what is described here is the general current of secularization of a so-far sacral culture. One may thus theorize that with a natural shift, the weakening of ecclesiastical hold on the enterprises of men, brought along the latter's self-assertion in every domain of his life and activities. However, it would be false to equate secularization, in most respects a healthy trend,[29] with humanism, since the latter emerged increasingly as a counter religion. Secularization was a lengthy and normal response to the excessive power held by ecclesiastical authorities in too many domains of the political structure; humanism was a doctrine, or network of doctrines, putting man in place of God and endowing him with features he was inevitably to abuse. While secularization would be hard to conceptualize since it represented a whole new civilization with its components, multiform attitudes, Humanism presented itself as an ideology with its language, strategy, and clearcut objectives.

At first, the sixteenth-century humanist tactics was based on the already mentioned "two truths" of Averroist origin, which neatly separated reason from faith. The tactic was to defend God's existence against the atheists by saying that this existence cannot be proved anyway by reasoned arguments, it must be accepted on faith and on the—diminishing—authority of sacred texts. This argumentation allowed the humanist thinker to propose tolerance with regard to all religions, implying that

a) all were equivalent;

b) it mattered not which one you follow; and

c) they were all based on a common core, thus on a "natural religion" of all mankind which could be further accredited with all peoples if only the fanatics of each were willing to give up the distinguishing features of their own creed.

Fanatics, usually meaning Catholics, would have to give up things that could not be proved by reason, thus: incarnation, resurrection, miracles, dogmas, sacraments, the whole fabric of the faith. In contemporary literature there appeared two genres, equally devastating for belief and doctrine: the *colloquia* at which Moslems, Jews, Tartars, Catholics, Protestants, freethinkers, Chinese, scientists, and so on, participate, concluding after much learned but also absurd discussion that everything that men believe is equally dear to God and that universal toleration is justified by the fundamental ignorance concerning the real nature of truth. An outstanding illustration of this genre is Jean Bodin's *Colloquim of the Seven about secrets of the sublime* (Hepta-plomeros, 1580). This is what two of its discussants state, giving the tone of what Bodin himself, a typical Renaissance humanist,[30] must have also believed. Toralba, representative of natural science: "If true religion is contained in the pure worship of eternal God, I believe the law of nature is sufficient for man's salvation. The oldest leaders of the human race had no other religion . . . and they left the memory of a golden age."[31] Senamus, the sceptic, who had visited all the shrines at which men worship: "I believe that all religions of all people, the natural religion which Toralba loves, the religion of Jupiter and the gods whom the Indians and the Tartars cherish, the religion of Moses, Christ, Mohammed, which everyone pursues with a pure mind, are not unpleasing to eternal God and are excused as just errors."[32]

The last expression is, of course, decisive: It means that for all we will ever know, religions are errors, but the sincerity with which we believe them raises them above ordinary superstitions. Cusanus, in *De pace fidei,* was merely pluralistic and tolerant, but he did not doubt that religion is a serious matter and that all believers must be brought to the Christian religion—after the latter accepts to make some concessions. Bodin, however, boldly calls all religions "errors," although also "just" insofar as all beliefs, really convictions, contain a valid, or at least a noble, element. The theme had been made use of before: Medieval critics attributed to Frederick II, the anti-papal emperor, author-ship of the tale of the "Three imposters" (Christ, Moses, Mohammed), and up to Lessing's play, *Nathan the Wise,* tales circulated about a golden ring made by God, and its copies, hidden and found but in such a way that the three who found them could not know which one of them, if any, possessed the original.

The other genre of humanist literature was the serious scholarly treatise, the best samples of which are Montaigne's *Apology of Raymond Sebond* and Spinoza's *Theological-Political Treatise*. The first, a near-contemporary piece of writing to Bodin's *Colloquium* (1575-1580), argues in substance the by then standard theme that God's existence, thus the Christian religious truths, cannot be rationally proved, in fact, that man, changing and unsteady, cannot know the unchanging God. Montaigne's conclusion, that man may rise to God only by renouncing his own means (senses, reason, spiritual and moral efforts) and by letting himself be uplifted by "celestial means," by a "divine metamorphosis," cannot be considered a serious argument, rather the automatic response of an indifferent man still living in a Christian milieu. Spinoza's response, on the other hand, is not automatic, it is the weapon of a far more radical strategy. The *Tractatus* is a demonstration that all the assertions of the Old and New Testaments are fanciful means of teaching a better morality to a rude desert folk. Prophets, miracles, God's law, the doctrinal teaching are clever, although primitive ways of speaking in a popular manner to people who would not have otherwise understood and obeyed. Yet, Spinoza did not write his work with the intention of clarifying the biblical style and unraveling the truth contained therein. In his view, the same mentality—the prejudices of theologians—was responsible for the writing of the Bible as the mentality manifested by theologians of his own time, of all times.[33] A reinterpretation was needed (today's progressive theologians term it "de-mythologizing"). The second reason for writing the *Tractatus* was the defense of philosophy against these same theologians and their prejudices. The third was to show (in chapters XIX and XX of the work) that everybody should believe what he likes and that the external organization of "sacred things" must be left to the Sovereign's decision in order that unity and peace be secure in the land.

Somewhere between Montaigne's time and Spinoza's we exited from the centuries of Humanism. The following two centuries lived their honeymoon with the new worldview, and the current of Humanism, although strong and for a while still distinguishable by its specific color, joined, or was absorbed by, other currents: libertines, rationalists, sceptics, neo-Stoics, Cartesians, fideists, materialists, deists, utopians, rosicrucians, Freemasons, neopagans, and many more schools, sects, cabals, movements and esoteric projects.[34] Nevertheless, the proverbial observer from Sirius would have been able to detect a central humanist ingredient in all this enormous intellectual activity. Nobody else except an inhabitant of Sirius would have, in truth, be needed to identify the humanist streak because the very success of Humanism, its acceptance into nearly all new terminologies, effectively camouflaged its continuing presence. No doubt, "God" remained somewhere near the center of the debate, not only of the theologians whom Spinoza had found full of prejudice, also of the philosophers, scientists, and other scholars. Even the scepticism of Pierre Bayle around 1700, had to "prove" itself against the obstinately present "God"-position, for example of a Leibnitz. But the noteworthy thing about all the discourses focused on the God-problem was that somehow it was no longer about God that the authors were really writing and debating. Pascal's penetrating eyes perceived this well in the case of Descartes. Monsieur Descartes, he wrote, introduces God merely to give the first flick of a finger to his universe. Afterwards, he drops God as something no longer needed. In a sense, Pascal repeated a diagnosis made more than two centuries before his, by John Gerson, rector of the Sorbonne and sharp observer of the professors' and students' intellectual joustings in the restless capital. What for Pascal's time was the conquest of the subjectivist method (Descartes began with the *self* as the only reliable foundation of knowledge worth being called such), in the early fifteenth century was the philosophy of William of Ockham, an empiricism reducing all being to what is perceived, emptied of substance, hence of relationships between beings, and denying the intelligibility of God. Gerson noted that such a philosophy catered to self-assertion in science while making faith appear unreasonable.[35] He tried to check its popularity by preaching a deeper spiritual life which would help restore the right relationship with God. In a way, Pascal's quasiexistentialism was meant to be a new method (over against the libertines and Descartes), aimed at achieving the same results as Gerson's sermons: a balancing of the "geometric" method with the spirit of subtlety (*esprit de finesse*) as a new road to reach God.

The point here is not whether Gerson and Pascal succeeded in their endeavor, but that in modern discourse, starting with the seventeenth century, "God" was used as a way of positing scientific schemas as ultimate explanations of the universe, its origin, its motions, its stored energy, its conformity to laws, its mechanical nature. Gradually, then, the scientific schemas turned into ideological ones because science was used, clearly beyond its scope, to justify projects of placing man, triumphant by his insights into nature, at the dominating center of the world-all. To summarize: "God" became a serviceable concept which, through its identification with every successful scientific world-image, contributed to man's glorification.

It would be an error to assume that Humanism provided a mere individual image of man. It also contained the roots of a new society since it is evident that the man who declares himself autonomous, a shaper of his being and potentially divine, lays claim to a different community than the one in which he lived in the earlier dispensation. The Third Age of Joachim and the ecumenic world-religion of Cusanus clearly contained the essential features of the utopian, ideal City that the Renaissance and the subsequent centuries would propose with a growing insistence. These features, however, had to be concretized, and even more, secularized, before their latent political nature became manifest. In other words, the "ecclesia spiritualis" assumed real contours as soon as it was reinterpreted as a "communitas fidelium," and then simply as an "ideal commonwealth," peaceful, happy, and harmonious because it consisted of ontologically metamorphosed, more-than-human beings.[36]

The ideal picture that the Rotterdam humanist, Erasmus, painted of such human beings was based on just such a transformation. If all those who call themselves Christians follow Christ, he taught in substance, there will be no need for the use of force among them; by right education they can all be induced to lead such truly Christian lives that force will be replaced by reason and brotherly love. Mutual friendship will animate the life of society and nations, and make the State superflouous in all but its purely administrative functions.[37] This sounds astonishingly modern, as if it were put together from bits of nineteenth-century utopian projects from St.–Simon, Weitling, Comte, even Marx. And precisely, this possible comparison shows that Erasmus was no mere representative of that famous Renaissance "exuberance" of which some modern scholars like to speak; he expressed the inner substance of Humanism, man's vocation to transcend his *status creaturae*.

Before and after Erasmus there were other Renaissance figures who made this amply clear in political thought. Whether in the writings of Machiavelli or Hobbes, who are the main figures in this respect, the line of argument ran like this: Christianity as a foundation of politics had proved a failure. It cannot endow human beings with self-restraint or allay their fear of each other. What Christians had been doing in practice, and should now admit also as the ideal, is to elect among themselves a Ruler and submit to him in every respect. It is false to say that they lose their freedom; they only exchange a "nasty, brutish, and short" existence (Hobbes) for the security of the well-run commonwealth under the king, a *deus mortalis*. They gain even more than that, argued Machiavelli: Christian morality is not only inefficient, it also divides the citizen's loyalty between God and government. By taking ethics and religion in its own hands, the Prince will elaborate a "civic religion" so as not to disperse his subjects' loyalties and energies but channel them toward the efficacious, world-centered State in complete command of its citizens' thoughts and actions.

The exalted visions that a Pico attached to man soaring toward the divine status, the high hopes of Thomas More and Erasmus for a Christian utopia, soon turned into the hardly camouflaged nightmare of brutish beings commanded by a "mortal god" for the sake of security and efficiency. One wonders what separates this project from contemporary totalitarian regimes whose ideology is based exactly on Hobbes' premises: man, an exclusively material being ruled by instincts and impulses, is to sign away his penchant for anarchy and submit to the master who offers him the security of unfreedom. Machiavelli and Hobbes, joined by Spinoza, insist that the master should be particularly in charge of controlling the "sacred things" and the external manifestations of what they still called religion.

By the eighteenth century the enlightened humanist minds were in agreement that the ideal society was just on the threshold and that only backward religiousness was suspending its arrival. It was a matter of urgency to formulate what was then labeled a "religion of reason," in other words an indifferent hodgepodge as colloquies like Bodin's and plays like Lessing's proposed, a "religion" shorn of whatever the contemporary rationalistic mentality could not accept in Christianity: a transcendent yet personal God, revelation, sacraments, incarnation, resurrection, the notion that the Church is a mediator between God and man, a moral law revealed by God, etc. Kant's summary of the whole question was proposed in three famous works, *Foundations of the Metaphysics of Morals* (1785), *Critique of Practical Reason* (1788), and *Religion Within the Limits of Reason Alone* (1793). The gist of his thesis was the following:

a) the "priests's religion" is shot through with beliefs

unreceivable by the mind;

b) there is a natural religion which responds to the moral imperative intrinsic in man;

c) "God" is really inside our conscience, but we must project it as an outside *numenon,* a guarantee that man obeys the moral law that, in fact, he gives to himself.[38]

Not only in the "enlightened" circles of pre-1789 France, among the German idealists too, there were great expectations of a radical political change, prepared in both countries by even more radical religious transformations in books, discussions, pamphlets outlining theory and practice. Such messages as Kant's "An Answer to the Question: What is Enlightenment?" (1784) had the effect of intellectual dynamite, the solution offered by Kant being *sapere aude!*—let us have the courage to think independently, a denial of all authority as if the world could begin only now, with a clean slate. When, at long last, the French Revolution broke out, Kant welcomed it, and saw in it something that, in spite of the atrocities and mass exterminations, the "eagerly observing world generally approved." At Tübingen where then as now students were preparing for the ministry, a group of "Christian Jacobins" came into existence at the outset of the Revolution, with such youthful members as Hegel, Schelling, and Hölderlin. Their program was to conspire on behalf of freedom, reason, *and* the Kingdom of God.[39]

Out of Tübingen were to come Hegel's and Schelling's idealist philosophies, probably outlined at that time in the conversations of the two young students. Through them and others, Tübingen also engendered, indirectly, the vastest intellectual mass-movement of the last two centuries which lifted History to the throne vacated by God. Humanism, previously compressed by Church and State to the small space of intellectual discussions and half-clandestine literature, exploded in a massmovement with the nineteenth century, thanks to the tolerance of liberal society, universal compulsory education, and, last but not least, the flexibility of humanism to adapt to, and absorb, other ideologies whose premises it shared. For more than a century, Humanism remained what it was already in the second half of the Renaissance: an ideology not merely rehabilitating many of man's nonsacral activities—this was accomplished by a legitimate secularization—but a systematic reduction of the human being to an exclusively this-worldly being and the discreditation, through science and politics, of his transcendent dimension. Whether there was such a thing as a Renaissance "enthusiasm," it is hard to tell; there is no doubt that there was an early nineteenth-century humanist exultation over the possibility of re-creating mankind without a "master" or, as Hegel put it, "re-claiming from the Outside Individual (*fremde Individuum*) the attributes that man had projected into him," although these (divine) attributes belonged rightfully to mankind alone.

Yet, by the end of the nineteenth century Humanism turned radically pessimistic. The phalanx of optimists, from Voltaire to Kant, from Condorcet to Herbert Spencer, from St.-Just to Bakunin broke down by the middle of the century, and although like paganism after Constantine the humanist creed survived and often prospered, its élan was weakened by those who detected the contradiction between man's happiness and his cosmic solitude. Kierkegaard, Dostoievsky, Burckhardt, Nietzsche, Camus, some of them humanists or affiliates of Humanism, were again looking for transcendent roots, although the certainty of not being able ever to find them drove most of these men to black despair. Their motives, however, had been in each case the fragility of man left to his own devices, and equally, the horror of the absolutes that this porous man manufactured to replace the discarded absolutes. This was indeed the kernel of "modern humanism's drama," as H. de Lubac phrased the title of his famous book in the 1940s: The impossibility for human beings to live without transcendent absolutes, and the tragedy that radical de-absolutization, never yet attempted before the eighteenth century, established in short order all over the western world. As a result, a number of questions imposed themselves on contemporary man with a tremendous urgency:

a) Are absolutes man-made or truly external to man?

b) Are they of a religious nature, or may any absolute do?

c) Do we invent absolutes only to satisfy an inner need?

d) Can circumstances be established (State, society, cult) where the need for absolutes would be abolished?

e) Can the absolutes and man's rationality be reconciled?

f) Is there a meaning to life if absolutes are abolished?

g) Is the need for absolutes a religious one? A psychological one? A political one?

And so on and so forth, on the tormented pages of Kierkegaard, in the bulky novels of Dostoievsky, in Burckhardt's historical analyses, in the titanic reconstruction efforts of Nietzsche, in the anguish of Camus. These men may be called anti-humanists; but even such true humanists as Sigmund Freud and Bertrand Russell came up against intellectual and existential obstacles which they did not know how to remove, although this fact may not have diminished their humanist fervor. Both postulated the imminent liquidation of religion: Freud, as a result of the sense of reality (sense of guiltlessness) restored by psychoanalysis, Russell, of the final improvement of economic conditions. To their numbers one must add, of course, the Marxists who maintain that the liberation of man from class-rule and economic exploitation will unlock productive as well as cultural energies persuading all men of the superiority of a properly organized scientific society above all the false absolutes of the past.

There survives, however, an irreducible hard core of optimistic humanists too, whose typical representatives are men like Schiller, the English philosopher, and John Dewey, the American educator. Dewey is well-known to the American public, it is on Schiller on whom we must now focus some of our attention. To Schiller, somewhat like for Nietzsche, the "death of God" means at the same time the vanishing of all absolutes. The questions we nevertheless ask about them should not be answered because they are meaningless. If not yet entirely, we may be sure (is this certainty not an absolute?) that with the passing of time situations will arise in which the questions that used to loom large on mankind's horizon will lose their significance. But already now (twentieth century) we have so many (relative) truths that our task is not to decide which one is valid—everybody has his own—but to secure that such a plurality of truths remains a permanent situation (is this not an "absolute"?). Schiller's own (absolute?) answer to the earlier question is then that Humanism is the plurality of truths and that truth is whatever satisfies momentarily our cognitive craving. But of course even these truths can be improved and superseded by new ones. Schiller does not notice that he disqualified his own wisdom because his truth, the humanist-pluralist truth, may also prove false tomorrow.[40] This is what De Lubac pointed out in his book, not as regards Schiller, but four other, much more formidable advocates of atheistic Humanism: Feuerbach and Marx, Comte and Nietzsche. They also believed that faith in God had been swept away forever, yet two of them were still alive when a no less formidable opponent, Dostoievsky, concluded that a society of human beings cannot be organized on the negation of God, or it will be an antihuman society.[41] The primitiveness of Schiller's position does not even need a new experience of mankind to prove it wrong: His fallacious reasoning refutes him adequately when he so naively puts all his cards on today's pluralism and proclaims it to be *the* truth. What would be the logical position of the theories participating in today's truth—let us say of Hitlerism or Marxism—which also belong to today's plural landscape, yet advocate one exclusive truth to the exclusion of all others?

De Lubac writes this in his Introduction: "Positivist Humanism, Marxist Humanism, Nietzscheian Humanism: much more than an atheism, there is at their basis an anti-theism, and more exactly an anti-Christianity. . . . These humanisms meet not only in the rejection of God, also in the crushing of the human person."[42] The author wrote these lines about thirty years ago, and since the end of the war perhaps a few more humanisms have been added to the ones he studied, although it is more probable that existentialist humanism, etc., are nothing but variations on the earlier themes. Whatever their connection with Marx, Nietzsche and Comte, these post-1945 humanisms are as insistently atheistic as their predecessors. Thus the question for us in the remaining section of this chapter is the following: granted the self-affirmed atheism of modern humanism(s)—and I have tried to show that this was a logical evolution from the earlier forms—how is it possible that Christians today flock to its (their) flags? More precisely, why does Humanism exert such an attraction on them? Why do they interpret the New Testament, the liturgy, catechism, mass, the psychology of faith, the meaning of sacraments, the person of Christ, Christian morality, papal infallibility and supremacy, the Church's tradition, the teaching magisterium, the place of clergy and laity, etc.—in the light of Humanism and according to its basic tenets? If de Lubac is right and Humanism is a denial of God, a head-on opposition to Christianity and an instrument to crush the individual and the community—then it is also a counter religion. How can Christians accept to serve two masters so totally incompatible? What kind of seduction do they find in Humanism when for sharp-eyed men, at least from Dostoievsky on, Humanism has not only been the embodiment of Christ's denial, but also a failure?

To answer this question, we must return to Hegel and follow the line that links him, if not as the point of origin, at least as a crucial phase, to the contemporary humanists within the Church who at present have the dominant word over the Christian's economy of salvation: catechism, liturgy, sacraments, relationship between bishops, clergy, and laity,

Catholic school curricula, matters of morals—and wide areas of Church involvement in public life.

It is reasonable to say a few words about Hegel at this point since Christianity made its first, unobstructed junction with the humanist tradition in the person of this philosopher, father of contemporary speculation even in theology. Hegel was a Christian, a Lutheran, and proud of it. He had been destined to the ministry, but the fact that he remained a layman did not make of him a like of Renan across the Rhine, an overt critic of Christianity and the Church. Thus, he was not what one calls an atheist; in fact he accused the *philosophes* of the French Enlightenment (Voltaire, Helvetius, d'Holbach, Condillac, d'Alembert, La Mettrie, Diderot, etc.) of being crudely atheistic, proponents of a bad theory and bad strategy since the latter

a) put the religious people on the alert; and

b) failed to enlist the concept of "God" in the battle against the traditional concept of religion.

For Hegel, God was not a personal Being, but the on-going and growing self-knowledge of the World-Spirit (here Hegel uses the idea of revelation but he distorts it), a self-knowledge effected through two channels: physical nature and especially history, that is through man's always deep-ened consciousness. The World-Spirit enriches itself with new knowledge in proportion as it engenders (the term "creation" is to be avoided) through the universal law of dialectical growth, new things and events—and for man, increased freedom. We recognize here a conclusion of Cardinal Cusa, as we also meet with the Abbot Joachim when we study Hegel's division of history into "ages," of which his own, that of the universal world-empire and the greatest amount of civic freedom in the framework of the Strong State, is the last and the best.

There are in Hegel's system two definitions of freedom:

a) absolute freedom, which consists of my not having set over against me anything absolutely other, but rather depending on a content constituted ultimately by myself;[43]

b) political freedom, the maximum that man can attain which is still compatible with the authority of the State; this freedom, however, does not so much manifest itself on the level of the citizen as on the State's level; thus, it is indeed the State which is free, in the sense of a), and the citizen merely benefits by it.

It is not difficult, in the light of various foregoing passages, to see the impact that these notions of God, progressive "revelation," history and consciousness as growth, absolute freedom, and the like, have had on certain Christian minds, minds similar to those whose attraction to Joachim's, Cusanus's, and Pico's systems was irresistible at a time when expressions of sympathy were easily censored and sanctioned. In our own time no such danger threatens the Christian Hegelian, although papal encyclicals have not ceased denouncing this philosophy and the other subsystems which it has been sponsoring for the last 160 years. Just as Hegel managed to "tame" the French *philosophes'* crude atheism, the Christian Hegelians attempted to "baptize" Hegel's own speculative system as well as the systems derived from it. The second operation, however, was unsuccessful; the one Christian thinker who saw early the implications of Hegelianism for Christianity, Kierkegaard, did not become a Hegelian; on the contrary, he devoted his life-work to combat it, although at the price of making of Christianity a near-irrational choice. Other Christians finally succumbed, not so much to the Hegelian system itself, as to the more recent philosophies which look at Hegel as the model.

The entire Hegelian endeavor, including that of his followers, consists essentially of the most radical attempt so far to transform the transcendent and personal God into an immanent motor of history, as such impersonal, mechanical and blind, except that some men, an elite, know its destination and are able to interpret its will. In this description, I have made implicitly a place for Feuerbach and for Marx, as well as for the legion of their epigones, most of whom concentrate on the "historical interpretation" part, not preoccupied too much with the problem of how was God turned by Hegel into a World-Spirit, thence into the immanent force of history. In this perspective, however, we can easily understand why some Christians think that their own contribution to the Hegelian-Feuerbachian-Marxian, etc., system can be a specific and important one. While all those non-Christians who follow Hegel implicitly adopt the equation: God = World-Spirit = impersonal motor force of history—the Christians insist that God exists as such, he is neither mechanical nor reductible to a motor. The problem for these Christians as both Christians and Hegelians is to find a formula showing that the personal God is not a mere providence, not an eternal Being, not incarnate and resurrected, not a curtailer of human freedom by his fore-knowledge, and not an austere judge deciding salvation or damnation according to an eternally identical law—*but* a dynamic-spiritual *Becoming,* identifiable with the historical *process,* one who (or which?) *grows* together with mankind toward a luminous, heavenly/worldly, utopia. The underlined words are the marks of the Hegelian orientation. The Christian adds to Hegel his own, badly mangled, prophetism, messianism, and alleged spirituality; but the Hegelian system itself contains a sufficient amount of prophetism and pseudo-spirituality (idealism) for the Christian contribution not to make any serious difference.

When he enters the Hegelian circuit, the Christian gives up his religion and adopts, although only gradually, the underlying humanist ideology. We have said that in spite of some ambiguities kept by Hegel himself, this system is totally atheistic. "God" was a projection of the best quali-ties that man possessed already when the World-Spirit was only half-awake in him, but *now*—the *now* of Hegel, the *now* of Marx, the *now* of Nietzsche—matured man is justi-fied to repossess these attributes. Man's God is man him-self, as Feuerbach brutally stated. Marx did not change the essence of this statement, but he provided an ingenious explanation for what had happened and why. Man did not himself project his ideal self into an illusory heaven, since this was not his own volition; he was compelled to do so by the exploiting classes whose interest was that paradise be not established here on earth, but only be kept as a distant promise, a goad for hard work and subservience before the slave's or worker's half-blind eyes. Thus, the slave/worker kept obeying "God," in reality his master's will embodied in the two most oppressive and alienating institutions, Church and State.

Why is the Christian impressed by these arguments? Because while he disagrees with their crude materiality, he sees half hidden in them a vigorous kernel of truth, and trusts that he as a Christian may be able to expose and refine it, eliminating the rough wrapping. The kernel that the Christian finds compatible with Christ's teaching is approximately the following:

Christ's teaching was truly revolutionary, making the Palestinian countryside rise up against the Jewish ruling castes and the exploiting Roman occupant. This simple teaching of poverty and love soon fell victim to Greek philosophy which transformed it according to its rigorous concepts and categories. The clergy and hierarchy did the rest when they grafted on Christian equality the organizational and political genius of Roman institutions. By the time the Church was made an official religion, it was a power–seeking and power–conscious "Constantinian" institution, arrogant with its Greek philosophical heritage which secured for it the respect of intellectuals in addition to the obedience of the populace. Jürgen Moltmann, a professor at Tübingen and formulator of some of the new theologies, goes so far as to detect a conflict between what according to him are two roots of Christianity: the oriental religion of promise and the Greek speculative corpus which insists, with Parmenides, on Being. This Being of the Greeks, Moltmann and his confreres argue, was transferred to the oriental/ Christian God, lending him its attributes of changelessness, eternal immutability, and lordship over a similarly rigid, once-for-all creation. The strategy against this idol must begin with a firm No; the real God is not characterized by the Parmenidian/Platonic "he is" (that is Being), but by the "he arrives" (that is, Becoming), the hope of the good news announced by the Gospels.

It is easy to understand, following the perspective of such an orientation, why Christians and Hegelian humanists (later the Marxists) were destined to meet at some point, and why the former concluded that a "dialogue," even a common course, with the latter was within the logic of their respective positions. Let us pursue this perspective as it is perceived by Christian Hegelians. A God who is not static like a Platonic Idea, but dynamic like the evolutionary process, could not create a static world, a static mankind, a preordained history, an immutable moral law and immutable dogmas. Disregarding the other subjects for the moment, and considering only the human being, it is thus obvious for the Christian Hegelian that man is incomplete and that he completes himself (compare this with Pico's view) in and through new historical configurations, creating and re-creating the world, in the first place society. Here is a passage from Moltmann's introduction to selected essays of Ernst Bloch, the Marxist philosopher: "Bloch's reading of the Bible does not begin with the creation, but with the watchword: *eritis sicut Deus;* and it ends not with God who has become human, but with man who has become divine."[44] Moltmann then lists the Christian thinkers who had attracted Bloch's attention and admiration, thinkers, Moltmann notes, who form the "subterranean history of nonconformist heretics," from Marcion and Montanus to the Cathars, Waldenses, Joachists, the Brethren of the Free Spirit, the Hussites, Anabaptists, etc. This is not only Bloch's preference for those whom E. Buonaiuti called the "ecclesia spiritualis"; it is also Moltmann's. They are the ones who taught, with more or less impatience, that man is incomplete but has a divine vocation, achievable here and now by the elect who organize the religious utopia with the other candidates to spiritual perfection.

The Christian Hegelian thus continues to run on a parallel course with the atheistic or humanist Hegelian. First God was turned into something mobile, then man, regarded as incomplete, grows in the direction of full spirituality or, as already the Abbot Joachim put it, *plenitudo intellectus,* perfect-divine-knowledge. The stages of this growth or divinization, are not necessarily running on the Hegelian or Marxist line, since as we saw, the Christian Hegelian or Christian Marxist prides himself on bringing an independent contribution—improvement—to their systems. Thus, the stages of growth can be seen, for example by Teilhard de Chardin, as marking the gradual, evolutionary spiritualization of the universe through which man becomes pure mind in the "noosphere" (a term that Teilhard coined from the Greek "mind"). But it is not too difficult for the Christian to adjust to the spirit of Hegelianism or Marxism either, as preparatory stages to the great religious explosion which is ultimately a great human explosion. As the Dutch A. Hulsbosch writes, "the man whom God creates is man as he shall be at the end. The men who are now alive in this world are busy being created. They have not yet reached the stature which was the intention of God in creating."[45] One wonders what was then the "stature" of the saints and martyrs who were nearer than we are to creation, yet regarded by Fr. Hulsbosch as more imperfect! Thus, the Hegelian process of the World-Spirit's gradual self-awareness is increasingly interpreted in the sense of Darwinian evolution; meanwhile the Christian jubilates in his discovery of a God who is not yet, whose coming-to-be depends on him and on other progressive-minded men. The general watchword is *away from* substances which, by being permanent, appear as immobile, regressive, condemned to ossification—and *toward* whatever appears moving, becoming, a ceaseless flux. Hope, no longer a virtue, is reinterpreted as a "dimension," synonymous with progress, revolution, a restless attunement to the future. For Teilhard, those who are not progressive and democratic will be mercilessly crushed by evolution which is just *now* shifting gears toward an accelerated "hominization" of our sluggish nature. For Hulsbosch, sin is no longer "the collapse of a completed work," as, according to him, the old Christian concept had it; it is "in the light of evolution . . . the refusal of man to subject himself to God's creative will."[46]

These new theologians, whether they hitch their instant-doctrine to the wagon of Hegel, Marx, Darwin or some more recent prophet, do not look very attentively at the filiation of their dicta. We saw that the essence of what they propose as novelty had been suggested by Joachim, Meister Eckhart, Nicholas of Cusa, Pico, and others. Hulsbosch on sin echoes William of Ockham (fourteenth century) whose thesis was that God is not bound by the nature he created since he has a *potentia absoluta;* in other words, he is as free as we found man to be free in Hegel's first definition of freedom. Consequently, Ockham and his disciples taught, much to the scandal of orthodox Christians like John Gerson, that God may alter "good" so as to mean "evil" and vice-versa, and that therefore a situation is imaginable when men do "evil" on God's command, or even that they hate him because he so wills it. The way Hulsbosch uses the expression "creative will" indicates, indeed, that this will may change (evolutionary) direction, and that today's Christian must be judged by standards different than yesterday's. We no longer connect original sin to a historical fall, Hulsbosch writes further, "we now impute sin to man's wishing to stay where he is, seeking his happiness on earth and refusing the continuing creative action of God."[47]

Enough has been said so far to make it evident that

    a) the new Christian thinker links up with an ideology of flux of which Hegel, Marx, Darwin, etc., are the outstanding representatives;

    b) he reinterprets the Christian religion (faith, doctrine,

dogma, history) in the light of this ideology;

c) he proposes the new amalgam not as an element for a free discussion in which he may be bested or ordered by the Roman magisterium to desist—but as a break with the "old" system and a newly revealed religion.

Proceeding in this way, the new Christian thinker no longer acts in the spirit of Christian patience, obedience, and submission to revelation, but in the spirit of the ideologies above mentioned which regard themselves as a radical and total break with mankind's past beliefs, experiences, and actions.

Let us now turn our attention to the concept of this radical novelty as propagated by the new Christian thinkers. Again Hegel and Marx, with the addition of a more recent philosopher, Heidegger, will put us on the right track of interpretation.

Hegel called the self-unraveling process of the World-Spirit "dialectics": The thesis is negated by the antithesis, and the synthesis is the negation of this negation, that is a step beyond the antithesis itself. In all these, natural and historical, processes of negation, not everything disappears of the negated phases; some of it is preserved although transcended (*Aufhebung*). Yet, we do not know what will be preserved; thus, while there is orderliness in the process, every one of its phases is new and incalculable: There is a break that understanding cannot bridge. Marx, dissatisfied with this element of uncertainty in his mentor's system, wanted to put everything on a scientific basis. The dialectics became, in his speculation, a material changeover from this mode of production to that, from this class-rule to that, finally from class-rule to the classless society. But he too was compelled to admit a break: the passage from history ruled by necessity to history ruled by freedom. Hegel had solved the problem by declaring that "meaningful history" had come to an end with the all-embracing character of his own philosophy! This was not very elegant, but it was impressive. Marx solved this problem by positing the "world revolution" which is both the result of a change of consciousness and the initial step of the new, "communist man."

For Hegel's and Marx's Christian followers and sympathizers, things are both more difficult and easier. What for Hegel and Marx were, after all, actual historical processes which remained historical processes no matter how these thinkers mangled them and falsified their meaning, for Christians it was a real stumbling block: the incarnation and resurrection of one Jesus Christ. Consider the difficulty: In Christian history the central event—incarnation—the drama that Hegel saw in Napoleon's potential world-empire, and that Marx saw in the accumulation of all means of production in a few capitalist hands—was clearly at a certain point of the past! It could not be metamorphosed into something contemporary and simultaneous with the Master Thinker, it happened in the reigns of Augustus and Tiberius, under the Roman occupation of Judea, with identifiable events and characters all around. Christianity is drawn to its point of origination, and this point cannot be shifted like the Joachitic date of the Third Age, from 1260 to 1290, to . . ., or like the Marxian date of the Final Revolution from 1871 (the Paris Commune) to some other hoped-for final revolution. Moreover, what Christ taught, his words and deeds, were not subject to change, they were not meant to "grow," to mean less today and more tomorrow. He even appointed guardians for his embodied words: apostles, bishops, a Church, a pope, and promised to remain with them to the end of time.

The great, the central problem for Christian Hegelians and humanists has been thus twofold:

　　a) to dilute the historical person of Christ and prove him nonhistorical;

　　b) to show that what remains of Christ and Christianity is a message which is reborn in every true believer, thus having no objective content fixable in advance by a Church.

The consequence is a process, a loose flux of enthusiasm (commitment) for the message, a future-oriented social fulfillment.

The gist of this three-point credo may best serve as a summary explanation of the most recent developments in Christian circles, specifically their "humanistic" orientation. Once this new credo is grasped, many things suddenly appear clearer: episcopal pronouncements on social or sexual issues, theologians' grave debates about married priests, abortion, or the ordination of women, the innumerable books and articles by priests and professors, the rewriting of catechisms, even the translations of directives issued by the Curia—and the uncritical acceptance of secular teaching and methods like sensitivity training, bodily expression, sex-education, psychoanalysis.

The process of diluting the historical person of Christ has been pursued, long and assiduously, beginning with Samuel Reimarus in the eighteenth century. Its chief representative today is Rudolf Bultmann (died in 1976), the German existentialist theologian, popularly known for his work of "de-mythologizing" the origins of Christianity.[48] This procedure of dilution has no apparent link with humanism, yet its conclusions directly serve it. For what Bultmann does is to show with an elaborate historical apparatus that it matters not whether there was or there was not a concrete person called Jesus; the important thing in the Christian religion is the *message*. The message of Moses, Bultmann argues, is addressed to a given nation, the Hebrews, but the message of Jesus is universal; its true outcome ought not to be, was not meant to be, the establishment of a Church, a doctrine, a moral law forever binding, but the personal and unique effect on every man to the end of time. The message, therefore, has no greater importance whether it was—hypothetically—uttered by Jesus or by nobody in particular. This is so true that one may speak of an "incarnation" and "resurrection" each time the believer commits and recommits himself to the message.

The popes have understandably condemned this theory and emphasized the concrete historicity of Jesus in the words "Tu es Petrus," and the charisma of priests to administer the sacraments; they called at numerous times attention to the immense danger when everybody is told that his subjective feelings, emotions, and enthusiasms represent the sudden surfacing of God in him.[49] This was already the belief of the Rhinish sects and mystics, this was already the object of condemnation by the authorities of the Jewish and Moslem religions. Today, Bultmann's interpretation enjoys a tremendous success because contemporary man is more inclined to take himself for an ultimate source of truth (the essence of Humanism), for a spokesman for the "God within." Hence much of what passes for theology these days is a discussion of the "new creation," the "coming-of-age of man," "God as future," man's "self-making" (the existentialist thesis), etc. Although this is still denied, man is now regarded by the new theology as an absolute, which accords not only with teachings of Hegel and Marx, also with the views of the pragmatic-humanist Schiller. When the latter writes that with the death of God, their model, all the other absolutes also vanished—except his own pragmatic—humanist one, we added—and that truth is what satisfied each individual's search for cognition, Schiller in fact suggests that every man should have his private absolute and be ready to exchange it for another when it suits him. Fr. Gregory Baum's statement seems to come out directly from Schiller's text when he writes: "I prefer [!] to think that man may not submit to an authority outside of himself."[50]

Man is thus the last and only judge of the divine, and the divine is not outside him, a concretely existent being, but inside him, and subject to change. We return to the notion of a future-oriented flux where, in the spirit of existentialism, past and present are abolished and man lives only in his tension toward the "he arrives," vulgarly self-fulfillment. Hence, the vogue of the theology of hope,

Todd Wehr Memorial Library
Viterbo College—La Crosse, WI

of the theology of revolution, of the theology of liberation, themselves subdivisions of "process theology." And process theology itself was spawned by the Hegelian (dialectical) unraveling World–Spirit. These theologians try to rest their case on the promise contained in Christ's words, which they interpret as existence having no essence only constant evolvement (again the existentialist influence). With naivete or bad faith, it is hard to decide, they focus on one aspect alone of Christ's words, the aspect of promise. But Christ preached to human beings as they are actually constituted, with their thirst for being and their leaning on past and present and future in equal measure. It is false to take pretext on the promise alone and dismiss what is called disparagingly "fixity." By doing so, one abolishes the entire message as having no content at all, and allows any fleeting emotion or ephemeral enthusiasm for a cause to take on the value of the message. In fact, this is exactly what happens in particularly primitive and extreme cases.

Even Fr. Yves Congar, the theologian who had most to do with initiating Vatican II, in other words a so-called "progressive" thinker, insists on "fixity" in the Church. He writes in his influential *True and False Reform in the Church:* "We are under the new and definitive revelation.[51] What belongs to it as its essence can no longer change and cannot be superseded: the statement of apostolic faith, the sacraments, the apostolic authority, in other words the priesthood, the magisterium and the power. Whatever structures the Church cannot be changed; it is given, it is final, it is not subject to reform."[52] Such expressions of "fixity" can have, naturally, no effect on the men we are discussing because, like Joachites, Marxists, or Teilhardians, they would answer that the fixists belong to the old dispensation, the rigid conceptualism of the Greeks; therefore, they cannot understand the significance of the new dispensation. This is what one of the most prestigious theologians of today, Fr. Karl Rahner, writes in an article on "Marxist Utopia and the Christian Future of Man": "Religion understands itself and can be understood only by reference to the future, which it knows as absolute and as coming to both individual man and all mankind. Its interpretation of the past occurs in and through the progressive disclosure of the approaching future, and the sense and meaning of the present are based on a hopeful openness to the absolute future's imminent advent. . . . Thus, the real nature of man can be defined precisely as the possibility of attaining the absolute future—not this or that particular state of affairs which is always encompassed by another and greater future still unrealized . . . and which, therefore, is relativised and known to be such. In this sense, Christianity is the religion of becoming, of history, of self-transcendence, of the future. . . . For it . . . everything is understandable only in relation to what is still unrealized."

Here, we have in a summary statement the dismissal of the history and tradition of the Church, but also of Jesus Christ, unless his message is interpreted in the confiscatory, Bultmannian sense. Other influential theologians express the same ideas in their own idiom, so that one is justified to wonder why these men, wedded to novelty, do nothing but repeat their own earlier statements and the identically oriented statements of their confreres. Take again Moltmann: "Man is not an established being, . . . he is open to the future, open for new, promised possibilities of being. . . . He can become what he is not yet and never was."[53] Or: "Future is God's essential nature" (idem, p. 16). Or: The resurrection of Christ should be understood "in the modus of promise. It has its time still ahead of us, it is a historic phenomenon only in its relation to its future" (p. 190.).[54] Or, let us listen to Hans Küng, a writer of theological best-sellers, Moltmann's colleague at Tübingen: "Transcendence is to be understood as Jesus spoke of it: primarily in the temporal sense [!]: God before us. God is not simply the timeless, eternal reality . . . he is the future reality, who is to come, who bestows hope. . . . This means for man that he cannot take existing things in world and society as definitive. He must commit himself to the reality of God which is ahead of him."[55]

Two conclusions may be drawn from the present developments:

a) The general tendency of the most vocal Christian intellectuals today, who are in a position to plan "nonfixist" reforms and impose them on the whole Church, is toward a this-worldly religion, which may in fact be taken for a correct definition of humanistic ideology;

b) in spite of the verbosity of the myriad presentations of novelties, projects and programs, the new theology remains notably vacuous; consequently

c) its irresistible tendency is to adjust to radically secular doctrines (Hegelian, Marxist, evolutionist, existentialist) and to slip insensibly into the language and premises of these doctrines, until it becomes indistinguishable from them.

The transformation from the "fixist" to the "process" theology, from one religion to another, is followed through with the inexorability of fanatics. We saw the new definition of sin, given by Frs. Hulsbosch and Teilhard: to remain fixed in one place, refusal of God's "creative will" to be completed in the soul, the refusal to take the next turn of evolution. In other words, sin is not to commit an objectively evil act, then to remain obstinately engrossed in nonrepentance (the concept of St. Augustine, of Dante), it is a vague nonconformity to what is supposed to be the direction of history. History is a fluid, formless thing even in Hegel's system; when Christians try to adopt it—that is those who ought to know that their Church is a mediating agency between God and man, working with faith, reason and clear common sense—it becomes empty of all meaning. How does the Christian fathom the direction of God's will for the "future," other than by listening to what God had said for all eternity? Since in the Christian view scrutinizing God's will in any other way is not possible, the process-theologian turns to Hegelian, etc., ideology in order to concretize his own vague futuristic propositions. Thus, gradually the process–theologian turns into an ideologue, and, since his imagination is uncomfortable within his religion, he pours his vague future–bias into the ready mold of a just then fashionable secular ideology. This temptation is not only intellectual, but also carnal. An alluringly bedecked ideology is waiting for the process–theologian after he had exhausted the mundane possibilities of his interpretation of Christianity, of sin, of morals, of real presence; the this–worldly kingdom can still not be justified on Christian grounds. He then comes upon a sentence like the following: "Thanks to Hegel, man has understood his essential finitude. This science as wisdom ended history because through it man has grasped himself as mortal, free, and rightfully thriving for non transcendental, immanent goals. It enables him to become action."[56] Clear, radically God-less, promising a radiant future no longer outside history: this is exactly the transposition of the Christian message into its opposite register. An irresistible trap for the man having no longer faith and hope in God.

One should not be surprised that, as said before, all the stable concepts of Christian teaching undergo now, at the Christian humanists's hands, a radical transformation. This leads, first, to their immersion in the flux which has the effect of a slow dissolvant; the second step is the abolition of the concepts. We saw that *sin* has been made into some vague non-attunement to a similarly vague process; this leads, in turn, to a re-evaluation of the sacrament of *confession,* indeed of *communion.* At the same time, communion is attacked from yet another angle: The *real presence* in the eucharistic sacrifice is denied; instead of transsubstantiation, Fr. Schillebeecx and the authors of the Dutch Catechism want to accredit "transsignification." Christ is no longer in the host, only his memory lingers among those who attend mass, that is those who "commemorate his sacrifice." They are told that, as modern men, knowledgeable in science, they cannot believe such a primitive procedure as one substance turning into another; truth is, they experience such a procedure every day as the food they eat becomes blood, they read about uranium becoming nuclear energy, and so on. *Revelation,* we saw it in Bultmann's theory, is also dissolved in the continuing process. "To speak of revelation as closed, is impossible. Given the denial of a transcendent God and the identification of God with the world, God becomes a process-God."[57] A "process-God" may still reveal his will, but it is then a changing will, a mobile truth, without any criterion other than novelty. And here again, since the will of God as such cannot be fathomed, the shift to a mundane religion (ideology) is inevitable: History or the Ruling Party becomes the source of revelation.

Finally, *God* himself is radically changed into something unrecognizable. This is the *conditio sine qua non* of the entire revolution enacted at present in the Church. If from man's point of view we define the monotheistic religion as a *coherent and sustained acceptance of nonidentity with God,* then we become intensely aware of the humanist theologians' project to cast doubt on this truth and move man gradually toward the equation: man is god. The strategy, followed single-mindedly throughout the centuries, has been remarkably ingenious: We cannot list here all the names that God received from those thinkers who would criticise the natural movement of the mind to call God God; their epigones call him "ground of our being" (Tillich, etc.), "Super-Christ" (Teilhard), "Future" (Moltmann), all of them variations of an old gnostic reference to the "nonbeing God." As if to be called *being* and to state of him that he *is* (the "I am who I am" of the Old Testament) were an affront to God, the theologians torment their minds to separate God from being and give an abstract abracadabra the role of a true referent.[58] This is the way how Hans Küng, for example, avoids having to call Jesus God: ". . . for believers," he writes, "Jesus came among men as God's advocate and deputy, representative and delegate, and was confirmed by God." Five references skirting the issue, and 720 pages to surround Jesus Christ with clouds of ambiguity.[59]

The humanist theologian (or prelate, or priest, or layman) should be regarded as what he is, a humanist, not a Christian in the orthodox sense. He has accepted or indeed initiated a system of thought in which not only the traditional image of God, man, revelation, incarnation, sacraments and Church has been discarded, but the canons of thought as such. In other words, out of the new theology—humanist, process, Hegelian, liberating, revolutionary, or whatever it calls itself—not even a new and reformed Christianity could emerge, only an absurd and idolatrous ideology within which anything may be asserted as well as its opposite. The words of Cornelio Fabro ought to have a therapeutic effect, if not on the theologians themselves, at least on their actual and potential listeners: "There is but *one* genuine notion of God, God as supreme Being, distinct from the world, a knowing and willing Being, hence personal, free cause of the world. A God conceived as an act of the world, immersed in the world, emerging from the flux of the world's becoming, as an immanent aim of universal evolution—is not a God."[60]

Footnotes to Chapter One.

1. *Histoire de la Philosophie,* I., p. 489.

2. T. E. Mommsen, "St. Augustine and the Idea of Progress," *Journal of the History of Ideas,* 1941, p. 355.

3. *loc. cit.* p. 370.

4. It took several centuries to formulate these matters with precision. It was the main business of the Council of Nicaea (325) and of the Council of Ephesus (431). The orthodox doctrine

58   CHRISTIAN HUMANISM

was worked out against powerful critics, most of them influenced
by the contemporary vogue of neo-Platonism of Plotinus's "theory
of emanations" (third century). Arius, the fourth century heresiarch, was also influenced by Plotinus; he held that Christ was
not one with God, he was God's immediate emanation, the incarnate *nous* (mind). The Church never ceased emphasizing Christ's
human *and* divine nature.

5. In P. de Labriolle, *La Réaction païenne,* p. 119.

6. G. Boissier, *La Religion romaine,* I., IX.

7. At the present time we witness the undeniable success of efforts indicated in b).

8. Using the term "pagan speculation," we cannot ignore for a
moment the immense and in every respect decisive contribution
of Greek philosophy not only to mankind's understanding of
itself, but also to the formulation of Christian philosophy and
theology. This is not the place to document, or even to outline,
this contribution. On the other hand, the critics who argue that
Christianity was a confused prophetic creed of the Judaic religion
before it received its theoretical formulation and conceptual in-
struments from Greek philosophy clearly exaggerate. Christianity
expressed certain of its doctrines in the then available terms of
Greek philosophy, but it did so with extreme care and prudence
as shown by its rejection of the bulk of that philosophy. Thus,
Christian philosophy is an independent speculative edifice, in-
corporating many elements but not tied to any of them.

9. *De Genesi contra Manichaeos,* I., 23, 40.

10. *What is Political Philosophy?* p. 71.

11. *The Mirror of Eternal Salvation.*

12. Several other factors also contributed to these later developments. Some will be mentioned in this Chapter, others in Chapter
Two. Our main objective is to retrace the humanist ideology
from its origin until today.

13. "What Joachim claimed was that his intelligence enabled him
to see and to understand the hidden meanings of the sacred
text and to discover in its pages the whole history of mankind:

past, present, future." G. La Piana, "Joachim of Fiore, A critical survey" in *Joachim of Fiore in Christian Thought, I.,* p. 11.

14. Like St. Augustine against the critics of his time, St. Thomas also was to reassert in the following century that no phase in history can be more perfect than the one under New Testament law, and that this will remain so until Last Judgment.

15. "Ecclesia Spiritualis," *Eranos,* 1937.

16. More of this in Chapter Two.

17. Letter Nr. 86.

18. "Apophatic" means "ineffable," the refusal to speak of God by giving him any name or attribute, all language being anthropomorphic. This tradition impressed itself particularly on theologians of the Eastern Church, but remained influential on western mysticism also.

19. M. de Gandillac, *La Philosophie de Nicholas de Cues,* p. 109.

20. *Ibid,* p. 163.

21. Compare it with the position of the authors of the "Dutch Catechism" who also teach that the Mass is a commemorative, symbolic event of the one sacrifice performed by Jesus.

22. It is false to assume that the Renaissance and Humanism were an epoch honoring the scientific worldview. With the Church's slackened vigilance, the Renaissance men and the humanists turned their attention to occult studies, alchemy, astrology, magic, the cabala, hermetism, sorcery, etc. The scientific method is of a later vintage; it begins with Galileo and Newton.

23. The seventeenth-century French scholar, Isaac Casaubon, was the first to prove that Hermes never existed; it may have been the pseudonym of a second or third century writer. With this discovery, Hermes' immense prestige as the source of all occult knowledge collapsed.

24. A favorite image of Nicholas was his description of how one thing is generated by another without real causality or external

intervention: the way the point "becomes" the line, the line a surface, the surface a volume.

25. It is remarkable that this was also the dream of Emperor Julian, the Apostate (died in 363) whose purified pagan cult, formulated to replace the recently victorious Christianity, was to be administered in the same manner.

26. *Pic de la Mirandole,* Aubier, Paris, 1974.

27. *Les Origines des sciences humaines,* Payot, Paris, 1967, p. 495. The Polish scholar, Prof. Andrej Novicki, sees Pico as the precursor of Bacon and Descartes, in search of a method which would "make of man the master and possessor of nature." We saw that it is not necessarily Novicki's Marxist ideology which dictates this evaluation.

28. *The Spirit and Forms of Protestantism,* Meridian Books, 1964, p. 152.

29. By secularization, we mean the outcome of the centuries long struggle of the temporal order to emancipate itself from ecclesiastic supremacy.

30. Bodin was an important and on the whole balanced political writer; a public servant; a judge who argued against sorcery yet sentenced one "sorceress" to the stake; an advocate of toleration and a believer in centralized monarchy.

31. *Heptaplomeres,* p. 225.

32. *Ibid.,* p. 251.

33. Letter to Oldenbourg, 1665.

34. The literature studying these currents of thought is enormous, a mere bibliography would fill volumes. Some useful works have been written recently by Frances A. Yates, Peter Gay, Ira O. Wade, Eric Voegelin, E. Gilson, Paul Hazard, Cornelio Fabro, Thomas Molnar, E. Cassirer, D. P. Walker, etc.

35. James L. Connolly, *John Gerson, Reformer and Mystic,* p. 236.

36. See Thomas Molnar, *God and the Knowledge of Reality,* Part III.

37. Fritz Caspari, "Erasmus on the social functions of Humanism," *Journal of the History of Ideas,* Jan. 1947, VIII, 1.

38. Kant was always fearful that censorship may deprive him of his academic chair. He was careful what he published and often used an obscure style to cloud his meaning. Only in 1920 were his much more outspoken notes published (by Erich Adickes) and even more recently, in 1973, did the Hegelian/Marxist A. Kojève unmask him as a "cunning old man." (*Kant,* Gallimard, Paris).

39. Such contemporary programmes as theologies of hope, of liberation, of religion, etc., were also formulated at Tübingen. Hans Küng is a professor there.

40. Schiller's main works are *Humanism,* Macmillan 1912, and *Studies in Humanism,* 1907.

41. *Le Drame de l'humanisme athée,* Introduction. (1943).

42. *Ibid.,* p. 6.

43. As summarized by Cornelio Fabro, *God in Exile,* p. 223.

44. *Man on his own* (in the original German edition *Religion im Erbe,* 1959), Herder & Herder, 1970, p. 19.

45. *God's Creation,* p. 45.

46. *Ibid.,* p. 45.

47. *Ibid.,* p. 49-50.

48. The best refutation of Bultmann's theses by an American scholar is Fr. John F. McCarthy, *The Science of Historical Theology,* vol. one. Propaganda Mariana, Rome, 1976.

49. This is how Pope Paul VI expressed himself on the issue: "Revelation is inserted in time, in history, at a precise date, on the occasion of a specific event, and it must be regarded as closed and completed with the Apostles." (Address on January 19, 1972).

50. *New Horizon,* Paulist Press, p. 52, 1972.

51. We remember that St. Augustine and St. Thomas (against Joachim) made the same point.

52. P. 146.

53. *Theology of Hope,* New York, 1967, p. 286.

54. It must be noted that at a later date, in 1972, Moltmann admitted that his theology was sparked by the optimistic sensibility of the 1960s: Kennedy's presidency, "socialism with a human face," Third World expectations, Vatican II, the sociopolitical upsurge connected with the ecumenical movement, etc. A rather flimsy foundation for a theology! Yet, Moltmann does not seem to have changed his mind in the less bright 1970s.

55. *On being a Christian,* p. 224.

55. By A. Kojève. Quoted in Cornelio Fabro, *God in Exile,* p. 624.

57. Edwin C. Garvey, "Process Theology and the Crisis in catechetics," *Homiletic and Pastoral Review,* July 1974, p. 8.

58. The separation of God and being is today a Heideggerian motive, extremely fashionable among Christian thinkers of the humanist type. For Heidegger, the initial error was made when Plato misinterpreted Being, making of it an Idea; later, Christianity adopted the Platonic Idea to explain what God is. Therefore, the two must be separated again, leaving God without support in Being. A "non being" God can then be anything; it is easily identified with *the* being we know best, man.

59. *On being a Christian,* p. 449.

60. *Ibid.,* p. 21.

CHAPTER

2.

Christian Humanism: Incarnation As Tension

We have seen that "humanism" is not a mere variety of enlightened thought, but an ideology, a man-centered religion. Already Socrates's contemporaries, the sophists, were controversial thinkers, not only because they had broken the rule by teaching young people for money, but also because they advocated a "humanist" ideal and taught that things are relative according to the observer's intent, interest, and point of view. In other words, that "man is the measure of things," as the chief among the sophists, Protagoras, formulated it.

Against the sophists' humanism, Plato proved to be a successful and deep prober of the nature of reality, human and ontological. Besides, the early Greek humanist thesis was contrary to the general tendency of ancient thought which held matter in contempt, exalted the spirit (pneuma), and placed the contemplative life far above manual labor. Platonism, as its overwhelming influence shows, met squarely the intellectual requirements of the Greek genius, whereas the "humanistic" trend, represented by the sophists, later by Epicureans and Skeptics, made only slow headway as a marginal movement, not conquering the intellectual class until the decline of Hellenism.

Insofar as the classical Greek tradition was antagonistic to the humanist thesis, the latter remained for centuries in the background. It was the rise of Christianity which provided a reformulation of the issue and removed the opprobrium attached to Humanism. The Greek mind could not conceive of a god unless it was infinitely above man and had a condescending attitude in regard to him, or even a mild contempt. The Christian concept, on the contrary, seemed to mix body and soul (the Hebrews knew no clear distinction between the two), and incarnation made it the

65

chief article of faith that God had chosen to assume the flesh-and-blood human nature. In this manner, humanness was not only expanded to mean nearness to God by right of similarity and special partnership, the functions and actions pertaining to humanness and to the human condition also became valuable in the eyes of God.

It is essential to grasp the import of this difference, the difference between Greek and Christian philosophy and system of belief. For Plato and Plotinus, writes Etienne Gilson, to be a god is to be a purely intelligible, living, and immortal substance. Human souls are so many gods, or rather potential gods which purify themselves toward a philosophical salvation.[1] In the Christian view, man is not God, nor can he become one. The separation is clear although it is bridged by God's concern for man (obviously absent from Greek theology) and man's worship of God. But it is bridged in other ways too. In one divine *person* Jesus Christ had two *natures: totus deus* and *totus homo.* In other words, the bridge is first of all Christ himself whose human nature is ontologically structured like that of man, but is perfected by its connection with divine nature. It is not corrupted like man's nature, it is not engaged in sexual and other relationships, nevertheless it rehabilitates human activities which are compatible with a moral and natural existence.

Thus, Greek thought emphasizes man's intellectual salvation through which he becomes increasingly spiritual, ceasing to be human, that is material and involved in the world of matter. His "salvation" is an open-ended one, a gradual rise above the human condition toward the divine condition, but intrinsically selfish as the distance grows between the self-exalted being and the world from which he withdraws. In contrast, the Christian's salvation has a goal, an end, assigned by another being who is not *of* this world but who acts *in* this world through creation, through his love and mercy. Implicit in the Christian salvation is the respect for the body and for matter, hence also and im-

portantly for other people's well–being and material circumstances, in addition to their spiritual care. "I am my
brother's keeper," the Christian must say, whereas the Greek
is not far from agreeing with Cain about the correctness of
a self-centered attitude.

On all these issues Christian thought differs decisively
from Greek thought, but also from the teachings of other
religions. With all his realistic account of man's life in
the material world, in the political community, and in the
domain of moral action, Aristotle conceived of God as
merely a supreme or first thought, unable to generate existence (create), but only to set the universe into (a mechanical)
motion. There is nothing about this god, or, for that matter, about Plato's or Plotinus's god, that would resemble
the God of Scripture, *He Who Is,* Who speaks to man,
using, as J. Pieper remarks, human speech so as to be per-
ceivable to man,[2] and Who has chosen man to be his
partner in the subsequent promotion of the creational task.
Accordingly, the Gospels are not a dry list of do's and
don'ts addressed to passive executants; they are a moral
drama in which man, a dramatis persona, is passionately
involved, endowed with a large degree of independence. This
view is not derived from a capricious, or at least arbitrary,
God, it is part of a rational thought-structure in which
other elements of the real world are also integrated. For
ancient Greek thought and for most other manifestations of
archaic thought, the highest good, the perfection, the supreme, archetypal idea are in the *past:* Man and his world
and actions are mere copies of a timeless and immobile,
immutable prefiguration. Consequently, in archaic thought,
as also in Buddhism and other oriental systems, such notions as time, nature, matter, human effort, ambition, man
himself are illusory images, and salvation is precisely liberation from these illusions and reintegration in the Great
Nothing. In Christian doctrine, Christ is, to be sure, a
historical figure too, imbedded in the fabric of human events
at a given time and place, but he is also at the end of

history toward which all must grow and improve. Nor is this all: If God had wanted to save us without our co-operation, Christ's sacrifice would have been sufficient to achieve it. The fact that he assumed human nature is a message (the *evangelion*) that Adam's sin is now on the threshold of abolition so that only man's faith and effort are now needed, as a supplement to God's grace, to ful-fill mankind's destiny under God's concern. The watchword for the Christian, writes Henri de Lubac, is not escape or evasion, but work with God and with other men. "The Church demands that we concur to the world's collective salvation."[3]

History, then, is understood by Christians in a vastly different way from that of the adepts of all other over-views. It is not the chronicle of God's acts through im-potent puppets, and it is not the meaningless agitation of material particles just barely aware of what is happening to them, but unable to influence their trajectories; history in the Christian view is a dialogue between man and God, a process with a meaning and with a promise, essentially free with an uncertain outcome at each stage. Thus, history is not the vehicle of a unilinear progress since free will forever hesitates between God's guidelines and its own decisions. There will always be war, St. Jerome said, and the vast City built by Cain will not be destroyed as long as time lasts.

It is false, as we see, to attribute to Christian doctrine and philosophy a lack of originality, to remark condescen-dingly that they are but imitations of Greek thought or that, as Nietzsche said, Christianity is "the Platonism of the populace." The two essentially diverge on almost all funda-mental points, because the axis of Christian teaching is the living God who was made flesh. This is how one can ex-plain that facing the slavery-based Roman society in which only speculation and politics were considered occupations worthy of free men, the early Christians engaged in all the occupations and saw the dignity of work well done, regardless in what area. The anonymous author of the

Letter to Diognetes (cca 120 A.D.), probably an apologist of Christianity, points out to a candidate to conversion that the new religion encourages its followers to become loyal citizens, blameless judges, disciplined soldiers, charitable masters, honest husbands and wives. Almost all religions and sects of the ancient world taught their disciples to despise the world as a place where the soul can only soil and corrupt itself and accumulate misery and suffering. Such was the message of Buddhism, Manicheism, Gnosticism, and also of the fashionable philosophical schools, those of Stoics, Epicureans, and Skeptics. Christianity alone asserted that the world is not exclusively a place of false values and of temptations to be avoided, it is primarily an instrument in the service of acquiring true values.

Our first conclusion, one of the two facets of the complex term, "Christian humanism," is that everything in Christian teaching, dogma, doctrine, and the philosophy built on them, makes us envisage the world and existence therein as good and potentially good. Since everything is a created thing, not only the visible world, nature, and man—but also intelligence, effort, time and history, the Christian's overall response to the world must be positive. This injunction is further underlined by the dogma of incarnation, adding to our understanding of what creation implies, the further confirmation of God's participation in the human condition and his redeeming of the world. Thus, by one of its aspects, Christianity *is* a Humanism, in fact it is the only acceptable humanism because the term does not then suggest a human being detached from God and cultivating his own nature as a goal in itself (the exact meaning of Greek or pagan humanism!), but a balanced state between two different but not antagonistic natures, fused at one point and one moment of the divine economy in Jesus Christ, the God–man.

At this stage of our inquiry, there appears, however, a serious tension which, when it is not allowed to remain a tension but is subjected to a "solution," endangers the integrity of Christian humanism. The latter does not mean either of these two things: It is not, and it ought not to lead to, the absorption of human nature in the divine, just as it should not lead to the denial of divine nature at the benefit of the human. The more important and prestigious heresies originated from an excessive, because unilateral interpretation of Christ's nature, some pulling it to the divine, others to the human side. The most notable of these heresies, at least up to now, was Arianism, which is so often misused as an illustration. The famous conflict in the fourth century was not between a Church insisting on Christ's divinity and Arius defending his human nature; on the contrary, the Church had elaborated conceptually a balance between the true natures at the Council of Nicea, and it was Arius, influenced by the philosophy of Plotinus, who emphasized Christ's oneness with God and his being a mere emanation, the incarnate *Nous*. The rupture of the equilibrium was Arius's doing, the Roman magisterium always resisted the two-fold interpretation, the one and the other inspired by conflicting tenants of Greek philosophy.

It is extremely arduous to maintain this equilibrium in the face of the gravitational pull of logic and of the other temptations of the intellect and appetites. The hard core of the temptation is both doctrinal and practical. Emphasizing the divine in Jesus Christ leads, as we saw, to the contempt of worldly affairs, of the legitimate needs of the flesh-and-blood human being, and of the similarly legitimate requirements of society, the body politic, of institutions. In short, such an emphasis leads to the spiritualization of all human endeavors, a kind of ethereal stance that contradicts the total aspirational world of the creature. Moreover, its consequence is what can only be described as *angelism*, which assumes that by shutting oneself off from the material world man may become more than human, exquisitely pure, superior to the rest of creation and the rest of men, not merely as a steward and caretaker serving the creational purposes of inferior and equal beings, but belonging to a superior estate.

The symmetrical and opposite danger is, however, to think of the human nature of Christ as having more weight than the divine; this view authorizes the shelving of the divine message as something that constantly diminishes for the benefit of the human dimension until it has lost its reality and is absorbed or overridden by the human. Fr. Yves de Montcheuil summarizes this position when he speaks of sacrificing the Christian to the human through the argument that Christianity was for a time "historically" useful, namely, while mankind was in its infancy, but that *now* it ought to be left behind as something detrimental to human intelligence.[4] It is worth underlining the *now*, because experience shows that stress on mankind's finally reached adulthood—when Christianity may be dismissed as a good or bad, but at any rate no longer needed servant— always coincides with the proponents' own lifetime. Various critics of the Church: Joachim of Flore, Lessing, Hegel, Marx, Bonhoeffer, at different times argued that although up until their own age (twelfth, eighteenth, nineteenth, and twentieth centuries, respectively) the Church had provided a useful guiding function to an insufficiently enlightened mankind, *from now on* the mature adult humanity no longer needs such crutches. Some among these critics, for example, Dietrich Bonhoeffer, say that God himself had ordained that religion should be a mere helping hand until such time that people can assert their own inner light. Others look for a historical justification of the thesis that Christ spoke of God as a symbol of mankind's collective *political* redemption. This view permits the reading of the Gospels as a revolutionary tract, and the interpretation of the critic's time as the moment for the decisive battle for utopia.

These two extreme positions are derived from excessive interpretations of what might be called authentic Christian humanism. It would be of the utmost importance to avoid what Fr. Montcheuil warns is a "split between the human and the Christian," as well as the absorption of the divine by the human or vice-versa. The Christian cannot have only personal preoccupations, he must act on the material that the world presents to him. Yet, when he so acts, and not only on lower beings like animals and plants but also on his equals, he risks setting into motion certain vices instead of virtues, impatience, haughtiness, indeed even angelism, so that the "humanistic" act becomes a direct denial of the warning that Christ's kingdom is not of this world.

Earlier, I used the term "tension" between the way we, when not adequately guided, differentiate between the divine and human side of incarnation. Tension only in our mind, not in Christ's person, but a tension hard for us to comprehend, let alone to live with because of its implications in our intellectual and practical life. Indeed, it may seem that this tension is fully displayed in what appear to be contradictory statements: the above-quoted one about the kingdom not being of this world *and* the injunction to transform our human milieu as God's privileged assistants in the process. Is there no irreconcilable contradiction here, one that invites our ingenuity to solve it? If so, then the temptation to solve it by leaning to the secular humanistic side may easily prevail over the opposite temptation, withdrawal from the world. At least, it prevails at certain historical periods, more activist than contemplative; then many believing Christians in good faith are swept away by the mirage of a solution. The hardest thing in such ages is to realize that there are no final solutions in this matter and that even the temporary solutions, bringing concrete benefits to whole classes of people—what goes under the name of social justice—must be guided by the hope of rekindling the spark of virtue, purity of heart, and charity. In other words, the divine nature ought both to inspire the action *and* to moderate its scope and its expectations. Maritain speaks very correctly of a theocentric and an anthropocentric humanism, drawing on a subtle and valuable observation. At first sight, nothing seems to be more natural than the requirement for humanism to be centered in man. Upon reflection, things will appear in a different light: We are so constituted that a certain indirection is salutary in our projects. Human effort may at all times be carried away by built-in enthusiasm, unless it is *not* directed exclusively at its manifest objective, but at one that is higher. Cathedrals, built for the glory of God, not for the comfort of men, are greater works of art than the functional office buildings. Anthropocentric humanism may derail and construct a system in which men are not only aided in their existence, they are also made to adore the human in themselves and in others; theocentric humanism implies a moderation, not only in the determination and carrying out of tasks, but also in the observance of more than the human elements. Since it is impossible to establish a genuine Humanism without integrating it to a religion, Maritain observes, and since (according to anthropocentric humanism) all existing religions must be by hypothesis excluded, it remains for such a Humanism to found a new religion.[5] The examples abound; Maritain himself refers to Auguste Comte and his "religion of the Great Being" by which he meant Humanity; the Marxist ideology is another illustration.

We find, then, that there is a danger implied in the term "Christian humanism" which is quite understandable since the adjective risks waning by too great an emphasis on the noun. What we distinguish as "primitive" and "radical" humanism are collective terms under which in past and present such classes have been subsumed as humanism of the secular, bourgeois, revolutionary, atheistic, socialist or Marxist kind, each of these adjectives adding something to the substance of humanism. The latter, when taken with a Christian qualification, is easily understood as the mixing of divine and human natures not only in Christ's person, but also in each man so that the collectivity of all men becomes, at least potentially, a kind of divine community—a conclusion actually reached by most varieties of humanism through the logic inherent in their position. This is why Maritain is justified in his statements that humanism is not detachable from religion, a religion it usually invents out of its own entrails. Yet, Christian humanism is not free of this same temptation, even though it finds a religion at its birth, and it ought to grant full recognizance to what this religion teaches about man, consequently about Humanism also. And here we come to the crux of the question: Because Christianity, in the person of Christ, is half-divine, it represents an obstacle in the way of Humanism's natural sweep. The Christian religion does not permit the believer to focus exclusively on man, he must divide his attention between man and God and reflect on incarnation as much as he may reflect on the human condition. In deep thinkers, the two reflections fuse, indeed man becomes truly comprehensible only if we see him together with his centeredness in the divine. It is tempting, on the other hand, to find this God–centeredness a distraction and thus to reject, or at least to put aside, Christianity until man "comes of age," "comes into his own," "becomes an adult"—until, in other words, he has solved his earthly problems. It hardly occurs to the advocates of this position that man cannot even begin to "solve his problem," in fact that this solution must derail, unless the effort remains inspired by the Christian religion, and not just parts of it, but of the totality. So in many cases the Christian humanist wishes to use short cuts, and after shelving his own religion he adopts another, seemingly more appropriate in the here and now, to fulfill his Christian expectations. It is an obvious case of using inappropriate means for a certain end, the more inappropriate as the means are themselves taken from an alien storehouse. The situation is, nevertheless, that the Christian humanist, from Machiavelli to the worker priests, finds Christian doctrine an embarrassment for what appears to be the urgent worldly task, and putting it aside finds and formulates a humanist religion. And since formulating one requires the study and the reflection of a lifetime, he usually adopts rather one ready–made, indeed one fashionable and popular around him. He persuades himself, of course, that he is capable of bringing Christian elements to the newly found creed, or that he sees in its tenets a great deal of similarity to the Christian religion—but this is a self-deceiving exercise because the secular doctrine—the ideology—he chooses is a self-contained whole which excludes and explicitly contradicts Christianity. The Christian humanist himself does not even notice the self-made trap into which he fell: His own eagerness to "solve the problem" implied in the Christian tension made him succumb to a momentarily adored public idol; he does not begin adoring it—and sacrificing his religion to it—because he had probed its wisdom, but because everybody, or those he admires, prostrate themselves before it. This is a long but ever-recurring story in Judeo-Christianity, from the golden calf to Marxism.

What is the deepest secret of the success of the golden calf as well as of Karl Marx, from the point of view of Christian humanism? The secret is that both seem to remove from man's shoulder the burden of the tension we described earlier. The tension was not invented by Christianity, but it was Christianity which brought it into sharp focus and explicated its substance. It is, to repeat, that man is both God-centered and self-centered, and that the tension cannot be "solved" because it is man's essence and the will of God. But why can man not abolish this duality and turn, single-mindedly, toward tasks that his earthly existence prescribes to him?—is the question of all humanists, together with Machiavelli, Kant, Hegel, Lamennais, Comte and Marx. The answer, as we saw, is that this is an impossible as well as an inhuman effort: Man's nature is dual, and if the aspiration of one of the two sides is thwarted, he becomes utterly miserable. There is an entire literature devoted to the lamentable situation of those men and women, who were forced to give up their worldly aspirations, for example, locked against their will in convents, religious orders, the hermit's life. There seems to be no corresponding-

ly vast literature, except for Dante and Dostoevsky, des-
cribing the misery of man shut off from God.

Nonetheless, the quest for the humanist solution continues and it will never cease; it is part of the tension.
Our century is particularly rich in formulations of the
quest and experimentation with it. The humanists argue
that the tension could not be solved in the past because
so far only individual solutions were proposed. But there
are now new means: technological, organizational, psychological, socioeconomic to solve the tension on a world-wide
level so that each man might learn from the other's example
and be encouraged by the other's enthusiasm. We shall see
later at what point the Christian humanist joins this collective enterprise, what are the arguments persuading him.
Already at this point we should observe, however, that
it lies in the very logic of Humanism, a logic taken over,
although distorted, from Christianity, that what begins as
attention and respect paid to the individual and his freedom (the first words that occur to us upon thinking of
Humanism) turns into collectivism, into a disregard of the
rights of conscience. This is evident: While the Christian
religion—and well-understood Christian humanism—tolerates,
even encourages and works for a rich secular life (Caesar's
domain)—provided God's rights are also observed—Humanism
in its problem solving zeal becomes increasingly intolerant
of even particles stolen away from its secularist enthusiasm
by a God-centered conscience not under its control. This
is why Humanism often becomes radical and collectivist, at
times indeed tempted by totalitarianism. This is also why
"for Judaism as well as for primitive Christianity the totalitarian State is the classic manifestation of the Devil on this
earth: The whole world follows the Beast and kneels before the dragon from which his power is derived."[6]

On the preceding pages what I wanted to present is the
issue of Christian humanism, with its two poles of attraction that other humanisms do not have: the Christ-

centeredness and the man-centeredness which are difficult to maintain in a state of tension. We now turn our attention to a brief history of Christian humanism in order to show the line of orthodoxy and the line of derailment, at times intermingled, and to see the various influences that have acted on both.

It would be vain to begin this history before the late Middle Ages. The only justification might be that Christian humanism properly begins with the controversies around Christ's two natures; but we have seen the core of the issue, it had no "history" as long as the Church was able rigorously to maintain the discipline of its magisterium. It is thus quite proper to discuss the history of Christian humanism when Humanism becomes gradually emancipated and no longer wears inseparably the Christian label.

The label is not even "humanism." The early ideas might better be called "secularization" and "laicisation"[7]; their thrust is to assert the separation and independence of the temporal from the papal, and generally ecclesiastical, authority. Medieval man, including the philosophers, did not think in terms of individuals but rather of corporations, orders, and institutions. It was not a question of endowing individuals with inalienable rights as we understand the term, but to argue for the freedoms of an order vis-a-vis those of another order. The interminable investiture quarrel between pope and emperor had awakened on the part of secular governments now advised by experts in Roman law, the ambition to emancipate themselves from papal tutelage. The argument was that the "two swords" were of equal authority and potency, in fact that Caesar's arm protected, and thus could exercise a certain control over, God's earthly estate. In the persons of Marsilius of Padua and William of Ockham, the cause of the secular power, more especially that of the emperor, found able and articulate advocates. The thesis of the first was that councils stood above popes, that they might be called together by emperor as well as pope, and that all Christians could by right participate, not merely the bishops. Ockham was more learned and subtle than Marsilius and used theological and philosophical points to establish his thesis. He proposed what in fact amounted to the Church's decentralization, division into provinces which would then escape the "tyranny of Rome." Ockham's proposal was partly inspired by Scripture, partly by politics: Since Scripture and Reason are the only authorities, he wrote, Christians can accept no doctrinal authority other than what flows from those two sources. And since Christ did not reject the Roman emperor's authority, in fact he submitted to Pontius Pilate and generally inserted himself in the Roman system, Ockham saw the medieval emperor, Caesar's successor, as at least the equal, if not indeed the superior, of the pope. His argument was that the security of the Church demanded that ecclesiastical abuses, eventually a pope's heresy, should be checked, removed, and punished. The emperor has the power to depose the pope! A contemporary scholar, Walter Ullmann, sums up the issue and the consequences when he writes: "Ockham hands the whole Church over to the Emperor. . . . Ecclesiastic institutions are merely expedients of policy and administration but are not essential to Church government. The pope is a mere executive organ under the Emperor."[8]

The point is not that Ockham was a "bad Christian." His faith was entire, and it was his concern for the well-being of Christianity which dictated his efforts to "purify" the inner life of the Church. More often than not, reform actions, even the excessive and heretical ones, take their inspiration from the desire to make the Church toe the evangelical line as the latter was interpreted by Ockham, or by Wyclif, Hus, Luther, and many since. Such reforms aimed at purification and simplicity easily derail, however, toward "angelism," and the opposite effect from the desired one is reached: in Ockham's case, the influence that his ideas had on Luther. The best Luther scholars, Lagarde, Boehmer, Lortz, Febvre, agree that the German reformer exaggerated the Ockhamist position by placing *sola fide* above pope and council, thereby opening the Christian religion to everybody's personal interpretation of the dictates of his conscience, with an accompanying depreciation of reason, doctrine, and tradition. Ockham would have violently disagreed. Thus, neither the early humanists (as we saw in Chapter I), nor Ockham envisaged the desirability and possibility of turning man away from the Catholic Church and granting his conscience full authority in matters of belief, sacraments, and dogma. Yet, the relentless denunciations of the Church, the probing into the nature of its foundation by Christ from Ockham to the fifteenth-century Italian humanist, Lorenzo Valla, into the extent of its authority, the shift of rightful authority to the temporal ruler—all this created the intellectual prerequisites for a re-interpretation of the meaning of Christian humanism.

It is then understandable how the picture changed with the coming of the Reformation, even before, with the shift of emphasis in Humanism itself by the end of the fifteenth century. It was still "Christian humanism," which means that Humanism was still engaged in a sui generis professional activity by believing Christians attached to the doctrines and tradition as defined by the Church. The Renaissance humanists too, the same way as Ockham a century before, wanted to bolster the Christian position, not so much by "purifying" it as, according to the scholarly matters which were of *their* interest, by reconciling it with the new scholarship and its findings. The enormous growth of documents unearthed, decoded, studied, compared and lovingly handled nearly submerged the Christian literature, but the humanist aspired to show that there was no contradiction between the latter and the new knowledge which came now to his scholarly attention from sources not always respectable. To be sure, there were the texts of Greek philosophy and others from Arab, Hebrew, Pythagorean and neo-Platonic origin, but they had to compete, like the writings of the Church Fathers too, against the mass of texts of supposedly ancient Egyptian, Chaldean, Kabbalistic, Etruscan, Sybillan, Orphic, Hermetic, and purely magic provenance. A large part of Christian humanism of the Renaissance aimed at reconciling all these traditions, and it is natural that in the process the emphasis shifted from the proof of Christian truth to the demonstration that men of all creeds possessed at least a part of the truth. The relativistic conclusion was not far to draw, but the time was not yet ripe; instead, Christian humanism concentrated on another thesis, namely, that man is a quasidivine figure, endowed with stupendous knowledge and secret insight into the nature and potentialities of creation, and called upon to change the world around him.

Pico della Mirandola was already in his short life time, and ever since, perhaps the most controversial of humanists who must still be called Christian—over against those who can no longer be so considered, the German Agrippa of Nettesheim, the Italian Giordano Bruno, the French Etienne Dolet, etc. But Pico himself takes his place in a chain of other fifteenth-century humanists, equally Christian, whose interests varied: Some, like Cardinal Nicholas of Cusa, wished to heal the four-centuries old schism between Rome and Constantinople; others like Marsilius Ficinus, resident scholar at the Medici court, studied Plato and the Hermetic writings and declared the ultimate superiority of the Gospels. Pico can be nevertheless singled out at this early date (he was born a year after Cusanus died, and was a younger friend of Marsilius Ficinus), because, as several modern scholars suggest, in his system man's dignity (in the famous oration of that title) is stressed beyond what his *status creaturae* would permit. The line of thinking is not necessarily continuous since Ockham's days a century and a half earlier, but the shift is sizable in emphasis. One of the most recent students of Pico's life and work, Fr. Henri de Lubac, defends him at all costs: Pico merely used the elegant form of Renaissance discourse when he exalted man over all creatures, but without implying an autonomous,

let alone quasidivine status for him. Another scholar, Alex-
andre Koyré, has argued generally that what appears as
unorthodoxy in Renaissance man's utterances shows only
the enthusiasm in which those times were so abounding.
Yet matters are not so simple. The problem of Pico revolves
around the question whether he did or did not maintain that
of all creatures only man has no nature, that is restrictions
and limitations. According to some critics, he taught that
man "chooses" himself, "creates" himself (the modern existentialist position), that he "contains" the universe, that the
freedom God grants him is not really a gift, it is a self-
founded indetermination over which man himself rules. If
man can be what he wishes, remarks G. Gusdorf comment-
ing on Pico's texts, then the explicative principle of human
destiny is not God's word, it is man himself: His values
have an earthly, immanent origin, and the world depends on
man's will. From Pico, adds Gusdorf, the distance is not
too long to Nietzsche who called man the supreme "value-
giver."[9] With this interpretation we are back with the
Greek sophist Protagoras and his "man the measure of all
things." On the other hand, it must be admitted that some
of the expressions Pico used were current in Renaissance
literature which mixed Christian verities with Latin oratorical
eloquence and figures of speech. For example, Cardinal Cusanus said of man that he is a "humanus Deus" and of
the world that it is a "deus sensibilis"; another prelate,
the French Cardinal Berulle whose orthodoxy was never
questioned, described man a century after Pico as both celestial and earthly, angel and beast, center of the world, "a
God, a nothingness surrounded by God, capable of God,
filled of God if he wants to be." The notion was widespread
that in all creation everything is endowed with a nature,
but that man has not yet reached the last degree to which
he is called and that the form he gives to the ultimate degree depends on him.

It is not our task here to arbitrate the debate about the
orthodoxy of Pico's humanism, but one may hold without

a doubt that for Pico man's goodness and freedom, an explosive combination were destined to redeem the world's imperfections. There is quite a difference between eulogizing man as God's highest creature (as De Lubac holds pico did in his *Oration*)—and making of him a mediator between heaven and earth who unites in himself the plenitude of the universe.[10] This is not just an excess of language, it is a decisive departure from belief and trust in creatureliness and providence. In Pico's view, God explained to Adam at the time of creation that he was made "neither mortal nor immortal, so that, master of himself, he should *invent* the forms he wants to assume; he might degenerate to the level of animals or, by *his own decision,* be reborn to superior, divine forms." (*Oratio de hominis dignitate;* my italics). If nothing else, this language is imprudent and immoderate and also false, since it contradicts our experience of ourselves and of history. As Henri-Irénée Marrou writes in another context, we are part of history's fabric, carried in its flux, at once active and passive because we both dominate it and accept its rulings.[11] This way of putting it does seem to restore the equilibrium.

The nature and thrust of Renaissance humanism changed after the Reformation had split the body of Christendom, although it is necessary to make room for many branches inside the humanist movement since those who claimed to be "humanists" were proportionately as numerous as those who today claim to be "intellectuals." Various Catholic scholars and bishops were humanists, but so were also their Protestant counterparts, a Melanchton, for example, or uncommitted men like Servetus. Paganizing magicians bore the humanist label like Agrippa, occultists like Paracelsus, polyhistors like Rabelais, Averroists from the University of Padua, apologetists of Christianity like Petrus Ramus and Guillaume Postel, and, of course, Thomas More and Erasmus. Almost all of them worked—and many of them pretended to work—within the Christian system of belief, although Calvin angrily remarked (in 1544) that "people locked

in their studies half-convert Christianity into philosophy"
and that the result is a turning away from God.[12] One
can hardly blame Calvin for his strictures against the various humanists and sectarians when one finds that Etienne
Dolet, another young scholar, suggested that instead of
Church one ought to say "republic," instead of pope "Jupi-
tor's flamen" (Roman priest serving a particular god),
instead of cardinals "patres conscripti" (Roman senators),
instead of the Devil "sycophant" (!)[13]

In spite of these manifestations of pagan and near–pagan
views, Lucien Febvre concluded his work on unbelief in the
sixteenth century with an acquittal of the humanists in the
matter. Indeed, while it is important to draw a line between
a continuing succession of humanists with a religious per-
suasion and the above-mentioned adepts of neopaganism and
gnostic heresies, it is more advisable to call attention to a
new cleavage and new problem that arose directly as a
result of the Reformation. Not only did Protestant thinkers
give a new orientation to humanism, they also compelled
Catholic minds to rethink certain articles of doctrine with
regard to freedom of will and grace, the relationship between God's providence and man's initiative. Yet, it would
be somewhat incorrect to call these problematics a humanist preoccupation, at least for another two centuries.
Fact is, the Reformation was essentially antihumanist; it
mistrusted the humanists' "paganism," love of Greek texts
(Luther scorned Aristotle and his readers), and worldly
endeavors, artistic interests. On the other hand, by its very
inspiration, Protestantism promoted the same objectives which
were increasingly central to Humanism in its emancipated
form. When Luther in 1519 affirmed (the Leipzig theses):
I want to be free, not a slave of any authority . . . Council
or Pope. And I will loudly and confidently shout what I
believe is the truth, whether it is proposed by Catholic or
heretic, approved or disapproved by authority—did he not
go beyond Pico?[14]

One of the main challenges that Protestant anthropology

represented for Catholic thinkers of the Renaissance and seventeenth century was this: Without agreeing on all points among themselves, Protestants from Calvin to Karl Barth hold firmly that original sin completely corrupted the human mind and the human will, and that God is *totaliter aliter* from man, unknowable by human reason. "When Barth recommends that we should not speak of divine majesty in creation without underlining at once and very strongly that God for us is totally hidden in nature, his words do not at all go beyond the demands of genuine Calvinism."[15] In spite of the believer's loneliness from God, Protestantism seemed nevertheless to strengthen his confidence in his own judgment that he can freely and reliably examine (free thinking—*libre examen*) not only the objects of his faith, also all matters secular. These words from Capitan's report to Farel (from Strasbourg to Geneva, 1538) are pregnant with meaning: "We have the Gospels, people are now saying, and we also know how to read. Why should we need you?" Concomitantly, the emphasis placed on the believer's conscience and freedom from tradition, authority, and teaching magisterium, turned this conscience into an assumed source of goodness, although on the other hand man's almost hopeless sinfulness is also stressed by the reformers. Third, another contradiction to be pointed out, which also turned from drawback to advantage: Since only a practically disincarnate church is recognized by Protestantism, one stripped of mystic attributes and of institutional visibility, the believer, knowing himself as a member of an invisible, spiritual body, accepted the supremacy of the State over the earthly manifestations of the Church. Yet, this very situation enabled the Protestant to work within civil society in such a way as to instill a large amount of toleration into the structure of the State, of which he is a more active participant than is generally the Catholic of his own commonwealth.

Against this triple challenge the Catholic theologians and philosophers of the sixteenth and seventeenth centuries' counter-Reformation reasserted their position that nature was created good, was wounded by sin, but that it can be partially restored by God's grace. Catholics were reminded that in contrast to Luther's theme of "fallen nature," St. Augustine found nature even in its fallen state so beautiful, great, and good that he wrote that had God created it in such an imperfect form, it would still be proof of its author's infinite wisdom. Similarly, Catholics maintained that human reason is not darkened by sin, it is still able to know God; and that next to a visible and richly institutional Church a vigorous State too has its divinely appointed role, both helping the believer-citizen to work out his salvation and his good life here on earth.

But under the impact of Protestant ideas (in France of Jansenism) and in order to counter them, Catholic thought began exaggeratedly to emphasize man's goodness, freedom, and worldly initiatives.[16] Certainly, not to the exclusion of God, but rather by leaving God out of reckoning, speaking of his function as "author of nature" (Descartes), but no longer as a sustaining, active, providential force. But, writes Gilson, the essence of the Christian God is not to create but to be. "He who Is can also create if he chooses; but he does not exist because he creates; he can create because he supremely is."[17] Simultaneously, Catholic moral thinking too was influenced by the debate with Protestantism. This can be best seen in the teaching of the Spanish theologian, Molina, which, according to Maritain, led logically to eighteenth-century humanism, separated from the earlier, still Christian, current. The Christian understanding was that God gave the first impetus to good acts, man freely consented to them but as a second cause. Molina divided the unity of the acts, with God and man having their separate share in bringing it about. Comments Maritain: "There you have the man of the Christian humanism of the anthropocentric epoch. He believes in God and his grace, but disputes the terrain with him; he claims his share in the matter of first initiative with regard to salvation, while he undertakes to construct by himself alone his earthly life and happiness."[18]

It could be legitimately argued that this is no longer Christian humanism and that in the seventeenth century there were no longer any Christian humanists, at least on the Catholic side, only apologetists like Pascal and Bossuet, and thinkers like Malenbranche engaged in the elaboration, and coming failure, of classical philosophy. The balance and the tension implied in Christian humanism could not be maintained, mainly because of the split in Christianity which turned attention toward the increasing number of controversial issues about man as master of nature and of himself.

Let us note, however, that until 1789 all the issues of history we have just retraced, as well as all the personalities, moved in the Christian credal orbit. Ockham and Pascal, Luther and Molina, Pico and Descartes, hardly questioned the faith and its foundations, and when they did this was still done in Christian terms. Thus, what administered the coup de grace to the Christian worldview and thus to Christian humanism also was not so much, at any rate not observedly, the conquests of science, but what might be termed the "social issue." Let us formulate it carefully. Neither the problem of science nor the social issue implies that there is incompatibility between the Christian position, on the one hand, and the scientific and social issues, on the other. But people engaged in scientific work and social activities do not stop to reflect on this compatibility and prefer to derive from their work an ideological system all its own, which they then oppose to what they regard as the rigidity and obsolete theses of the Christian position. The consequence was that . a false dichotomy began to be perceived between the "scientific" worldview and the Catholic religion, and later between the "social question" and Christianity. Thus, humanism, which was never actually Christian—only there were Christians who were humanists—received a new interpretation as the opposite of Christianity, a kind of modern religion, at least a substitute religion.

The dichotomy was further sharpened so that in contemporary times, in the nineteenth and twentieth centuries, one is either a Christian or a humanist. The first are labeled backward, immobilist and dogmatic, the second progressive, dynamic, and blessed with an open mind. In the nineteenth century, the accent was on the gap that supposedly existed between religion and science; the picture has been modified in this century because science has showed its terrifying aspects too: The new conflict is formulated as being between religion and social justice.

Quite understandably, there are many Christians now, as there were in the humanistic period of the Renaissance, who wish to close this alleged gap between their religion and the issue of the day, this time, social justice. Since the old regime everywhere came to an end, charity, help to the poor, care for misery ceased being exclusively the Church's concern (or that of the parish) and acquired a dimension of their own. Political parties, labor unions, the Welfare State itself monopolize these concerns ever since the industrial revolution has come to present material need on the scale of a new magnitude and as a self-contained problem. To deal with the problem, to research it, write about it, militate for its solution, etc., means today to be a "humanist," that is almost by definition not a Christian. The temptation is thus strong for Christians to "join the modern world" by espousing its central concern, and becoming, once again, Christian humanists. Consequently, the old danger arises in a new garb, in fact so much so that those involved are often unable to see the recurrence of the same pattern and argue that this is now an entirely new issue having nothing to do with the *tension* between God's kingdom and man's. They assert that these two overlap, in fact that what Christ himself meant by his kingdom was really and exclusively the this–worldly one. Deep and subtle analyses of this position, like that of Fr. Montcheuil, are hardly appreciated, even understood. The Church, he writes, teaches that authority is necessary in the State, but it does not specify the exact form it should take. The Christian ought to ask himself which authority seems best in the concrete circumstances of time and place, most compatible to fulfill the functions that Catholic doctrine assigns to authority.[19] What Montcheuil says about authority in the State is valid also for other forms of authority and for institutions in general. The Christian is not to espouse one definite type and, in a way, consecrate it as the "Christian way"; while taking his share in the alleviation of suffering, he ought to remain detached from specific systems, free even with regard to those institutions that came into existence partly through his own cooperation. The Church's social doctrine consists of a set of principles, not of a concrete plan of detailed organization for society. Yet the danger is, writes Fr. Montcheuil, that certain people with an enthusiastic temperament may feel committed to Christianity more because of what it achieves in the temporal order than what it promises for the soul in eternity.[20] A very profound observation, indeed, as it points to the temptation of "solving the tension." Just as four or five centuries ago, the Christian feels that the time has come to show his concern for the world, and he feels embarrassed that the Church to which he is sincerely attached, has neglected to do so. In a way, he wants to step in for what he regards has been a historic failure, and hopes to bring the whole Church to the understanding that he himself has reached. What Fr. Montcheuil says is that it is the Church, not its critic no matter how zealous and honest, which is right; and we add that the Church is right because no matter what any new ideology may temporarily achieve, its imperfections will soon prevail, as will also its basically secular orientation. Does this mean that immobility is the safe thing to recommend and approve? Hardly. As Montcheuil puts it, there is always an inadequacy between what human (social) relations are and what they ought to be. It is just and necessary to work from the level of the first to reach the level of the second; yet, not by joining an ideological system, another flag, because such a system either starts or ends up with formulating its own religion. Human beings cannot act meaninglessly; they are always intent on harmonizing their actions within one systematic whole.

Now since roughly 1789, the Christian has seen rise before his eyes a number of such systems which (a) seem to share his concern for the world's suffering, (b) promise and prompt actions seemingly more efficacious than his own under Christian auspices, and (c) claim to do so in the name of rival convictions which possess a quasireligious impact. Hence, arises the Christian's modern dilemma: *Either* remain a Christian but join these rival systems and attempt to "Christianize" them, *or* work within his own "system," the Christian religion and church, and persuade it of the importance of imitating the other systems and their efficacy. There is a third way, too, but it does not properly belong to our discussion: Should the Christian leave his religion and adopt the other system—even if only temporarily, until certain conditions are fulfilled? The third way is by definition not Christian, although the apostasy it implies may cause crises of conscience and a great deal of inner struggle. Thus, only the first two ways fit the description of the Christian humanist choice.

In considering this dilemma, we should appreciate its magnitude. Up until modern times the Christian religion and world-concept were often and savagely assailed, but behind the attacks there were only groups of scholars or secular princes, whether inside or outside the Church. It all seemed like a family quarrel, weighted in favor of the Christian religion because facing it there was no power proposing another religion, let alone atheism. There were only religious sects or a secular sect like Freemasonry. The new phenomenon of modern times is the appearance of the secular State and secular society. At the beginning, this State was not proposing an active antireligious struggle (with the brief exception of the revolutionary regime in France), it only encouraged by its indifference the militant anti-Christian forces within society. Gradually, however, particularly in the twentieth century, the secular State turned militantly atheistic—under totalitarian regimes, but also under liberal regimes where atheism takes on more subtle aspects, as, for example, in the form of laws legalizing abortion, sex education, and various activities of a clearly immoral nature.

This State has itself become an exponent of humanism, insofar as it is an immense and bureaucratically organized "counterchurch," in the name of a total freedom of conscience and, more spectacularly, of social justice which it monopolizes. Nothing is more natural than the Christian's temptation in these circumstances to transfer part of his loyalty—the active, militant part—to this counterchurch or to one of the (political) parties and isms which constitute it and promote its secular creed. He thus insensibly goes from one credal orbit to another, opting for what could be only described as a "Christian secularism." This is no longer the Christian tension between the two kingdoms, the accent here is squarely placed on Caesar's estate; the terminology used is still reminiscent of Christian verities, but emptied of their content.

As this Christian secularism[21] develops and grows under the shelter of the secular State and its ideology, it is, at the beginning, not as blatant in its *prises de position* and statements as the rival positions and statements, those of Marxism, the ideology of John Dewey, or the Humanist Manifesto, etc. As explained before, the initial assent is hardly perceptible: Of the "incarnate Christ" the first term is emphasized, the second term is used for the reinforcement and authentification of the first. The action which is undertaken on the secular plane receives its confirmation on the plane of the divine, but rather as one hastily stamps a document in compliance with regulations. Let us remember a similar demarche, that of Descartes: His intention was to explain the world scientifically to the sceptics, so that in the end God was merely used to indicate how the world came into existence. But this was not the issue; it was only incidental to the main concern which, without negating the main issue, reduced it to insignificance. At the outset, such a procedure seems of secondary importance; its veritable import becomes gradually visible and in retrospect, decisive. At any rate, the corporate nature of the Christian religion and Church would make it extremely difficult to emphasize individual man as the center of modern humanism; consequently, the Christian humanist focuses, correctly, on the social dimension, finding legitimation for his enterprise in the controversial thesis that God created the world with the intention of bringing it up to his own standard. For Pico della Mirandola man was an unfinished creature who constructs himself as a self-sculpted statue; this conception corresponded to Renaissance individualism. Pico's modern descendents speak in social terms: They see mankind collectively forging its destiny, after an initial act of creation. Just as Pico fell into near–heretical exaggerations (actually heretical, according to such scholars as Eugenio Garin, G. Gusdorf, Frances Yates), a similar temptation exists for contemporary Christian humanists, namely, to take out pages from the book of secular humanism and other ideologies and sprinkle them with holy water. Prudence in the matter is less and less popular, the kind H. I. Marrou recommends: "Christianity is oriented toward the building of God's Kingdom; it is not destined to help us organize the earthly city; it is not meant to be a force for the revolution."[22]

Such is the background against which we must examine the contemporary path of Christian humanism. Let us choose as its first illustration the German pastor Dietrich Bonhoeffer, whose impact on today's religious thinking is so very strong. There is a kind of historico–philosophical overview in Bonhoeffer's works, showing the maturation of modern man and the accompanying phenomenon of God's retreat from the modern world—the theme, as we saw, in Pico already. We may call the process described by Bonhoeffer "secularization": reason's victory over faith, that of moral principles over divine law, that of the universe conceived as a self-run mechanism rather than one created and informed by providence, etc. At one point of this process it was found by the philosophers (first clearly stated by Kant) that God is beyond experience, by which they meant scientifically verified experience, so that man could turn with a good conscience away from "metaphysical" speculations and concentrate on the transformation of this world into a well-organized and comfortable place. Hegel expressed best this conclusion, asserting that freedom consists in man not having over him anything which is *absolutely other* but rather depending on a content constituted ultimately by himself.[23]

The consequence that Bonhoeffer derives from secularization is not that a certain historical form of thought prevailed for centuries over another one, and may, therefore, wane and yield, but that this is the irresistible course of history. It is then better for the Christian to accommodate himself with this course because it is obviously prescribed by providence: God now wants to withdraw from the world and wants man to take over. If Bonhoeffer's thesis were appropriately scrutinized by independent-minded Catholics, they would find here a grievous contradiction. Ockham in the fourteenth century used to maintain that God's freedom and power are so infinite (*potentia absoluta*) that were he suddenly to intervert good and evil and assign the contrary value to each, men would start paying hommage to evil as they have done so far to goodness. The latter is not unchangeable in itself, it is "good" only because God had so ordered it (*bonum quia volitum*). Catholic doctrine holds, on the other hand, that God is not playing with us; *good* is what it is because such is the eternal moral law. In other words, Bonhoeffer is mistaken in his central thesis when he assumes that God "withdraws" now from the world. This is contrary to the whole concept of creation, further emphasized by Christ's promise to remain with his Church to the end of times.

For Bonhoeffer, however, it is now an unavoidable fact

that the Christian must plunge into a Godless world. In his prison he wrote: "It is not some religious act which makes a Christian what he is, but participation in the suffering of God in the life of the world;" (July 18, 1944). Christianity does not lead to salvation, such a thing, Bonhoeffer says, does not figure in the Old Testament. Christian life means participation in the world's suffering. There still remains the question of how we are to differentiate between a Christian and, let us say, an agnostic social worker, or an atheist communist militant, both of whom also participate in the world's misery. So do a physician, a nurse, a defense lawyer, a policeman. Are they all, by this mere fact, Christians? Are they all working for the Kingdom of God, for the salvation of souls?

One of two things: *Either* it is not essential to work for these objectives, *or* merely by participation in the world's suffering we work anyway for them. In both cases the accent is on one pole of the tension, the kingdom of this world, the *civitas terrena,* and the tension is dissolved, God's Kingdom being absorbed in the earthly one. This, however, is not perceived by Bonhoeffer and his followers. Christian writers have been urging, notes M. Jarrett-Kerr, that far from bemoaning the arrival of the secular society, Christians should rejoice at it for it is able to produce, more efficiently and professionally, the basis for the good life which Christian societies in the past have hoped to produce but failed.[24] Bonhoeffer's heroic plunge in a Godless and suffering world is here reduced to a kind of tolerance-*cum*-comfort situation, and one wonders if by "secular society" the writers mentioned by Jarrett-Kerr do not mean simply the representatives of the industrial–consumer society. In every period the temptation of those who abandon transcendence is great to regard as an ideal, as the best of possible worlds, the one in which they themselves live, with perhaps some minor adjustments. We find today a large number of theologians who equate the Christian religion with a selection of fashionable reform movements ranging from the inoccuous to the revolutionary. The "mis-

sion to the world" is not then understood in the apostolic
sense, but platitudinously as an injunction to be a jolly
good fellow, eventually a stylish dresser, an unembarrass-
ing companion who does not offend by reminding his fellow
human beings of a life dedicated to a transcendant and
personal God.

It is virtually impossible at this stage to obtain more than
vague allusions about the "mission to the world." Even as
serious a theologian as Fr. Bernard Häring is content to
speak of a "decisive being in the world," of an "active
life in the world," of "man engaged in concrete decision-
making," of "following the spirit not the letter," etc. It
is understandable that so much tactful beating around the
bush (so as not to offend the Marxists, the ecumenic spirit,
the atheists, the politicians, the rebellious clergy, etc.) finds
itself disarmed when faced with the concrete and boldly
asserted program of political parties, labor unions, academic
leftists, and representatives of the media. It is then assumed
that one may best "join the world" by adopting the fashionable programs, since, after all, they seem to speak in the
name of the large numbers, or at least of the noisiest ones.
Such a step suggests, of course, that the essence of Christianity has been allowed to evaporate and a kind of ideal
Christianity substituted for it, which is not concretized either
through history (tradition) or through doctrine. As against
these two, Christianity is then projected into the future
where it is supposed to become embodied in a manner
impossible to describe except in the words of today's politi-
cal-ideological expectations.

This is then the real nature of the temptation, the *politi-
zation of the Gospel message.* It is extremely hard to resist
it because, as we have seen from the beginning of this
chapter, Christianity is the opposite of a world-denying religion; it does not reduce time, effort, and worldly aspirations
to the status of illusions; on the contrary, it rehabilitates
work, history, and the State to their rightful positions. Yet,
as Maritain, Montcheuil, Marrou, and others have said

untiringly, the earthly kingdom, while fully valid, is not the Christian's main objective. Those whom we called the "purists" or "angelists" misinterpret this position which contains a Yes and a No, an affirmation of politics as good and its negation as first in the hierarchy of things. The Ockhamist ideal, so popular today under many insufficiently identified labels, is the abolition of both State and Church, that is of institutions because they are obstacles to the spontaneous love of God and brotherhood of men. The message is that there ought not to be either a spiritual or a civil organization of the faithful.

Such an angelism is seemingly at the opposite pole from what I described as the Christian humanist temptation to dismiss the church and join—or collaborate with—aggressively secular social movements. The opposition is less than genuine, and angelism often turns into political activism—in case, that is, when an ideological movement is able to convince the Christian that it is antipolitical, purely "human" or "humanist," even secular-evangelical. Having looked around himself, the Christian humanist has found corruption, abuse and misery. He investigates and locates the causes in the system itself, and finds in addition that his own church is part of the condemned system. The conclusion he draws is at hand: Only from outside the system can one change it, and from what he finds outside he naturally chooses the more radical and impactful battering rams. This does not mean that he has discarded his "angelism"; he has temporarily shelved it while descending into the political arena to combat, if necessary, with less than pure weapons. The main thing is that he does not lose the objective from sight. His conscience remains pure.

This is what happened to the Christians connected with the *Esprit* group in France, beginning with the 1930s. Their case is as symptomatic as that, a decade later, of Bonhoeffer, the difference being explicable perhaps by the fact that the latter was a German Protestant, the former were French Catholics. Accordingly, Bonhoeffer's temptation was to start from his own individual conscience which decided, like Luther before him, that man's relations with God must be placed now on new foundations, presumably because Christians allowed a horrible war to take place, without opposing it *en masse*. The *Esprit* group, communitarian like the Church to which the majority of the members belonged, assigned to itself the objective of reforming society and its class-relationships, and thus to bring the working class, alienated from the Church, back to organic relationship with the faith.

This was a commendable enterprise of priests and laymen. From the beginning the discussion centered on the state of Christianity in the modern world infected by the bourgeois spirit. The founders, members, and sympathizers, Mounier, Maritain, Deléage, Izard, Rougemont, etc., agreed that the Christian message was an otherworldly one, and they deplored that the bourgeois mentality destroys the effectiveness of the message when it identifies the bourgeois interests with those of the Church. The masses (workers) would not and could not be reintegrated to the Church as long as their class enemies seemed to occupy the pews. This was the basic thesis of the *Esprit* group, the same as that of many contemporary movements in Europe and South America, out of which after World War II the Christian-democratic and Christian–socialist parties emerged in France, Italy, Germany, Venezuela, Chile and elsewhere. This subsequent politicization was, strictly speaking, absent from the inspiration and initial expressions. "I feel deeply that the Catholic community is on the way to paganization," wrote Emmanuel Mounier in 1934. "With it alone nothing can be done today. . . . My best friends are nonbelievers. . . . The *axis of my vocation* is to bring about collaboration between the two groups."[25] Two years later, we find Mounier a little farther on the road as it always happens to those who measure other people's willingness to follow them with the yardstick of their own impatience. In a statement-report prepared for the Archbishop of Paris, Mounier writes as follows: "We have formed the *Esprit*-group in order to pull our Christianity out of the kind of ghetto where the chief organizers of the new civilization try to push it back, and to have it reincarnate in all the problems of our time. . . . All our effort tends to liberate the human person from the individualist errors, and the community from the collectivist errors.''[26] This amounts to the undisputable rejection both of capitalism and communism, and to the dismantling of gigantic and centralized economic institutions, whether run by individuals or by the State. These were positive projects. Yet, the potential excesses were not far as the heat of the battle increased. Mounier with his personalist philosophy of property compared Proudhon's nineteenth century anarcho-socialists to the Fathers of the Church, and called property, as Proudhon a century before, "theft" if it means the private appropriation of riches from the communally produced superfluity of goods.[27]

It would be senseless to demand of a group of Christians not to listen to the winds of doctrine in the world around them. Thus, senseless to ask of Mounier to deny the influence on him of Proudhon and other socialist thinkers. The risk, as pointed out repeatedly, is, however, that the Christian humanist in his impatience reaches for radical contemporary proposals and solutions, and far from dominating, even criticizing them, becomes submerged by their universe of discourse and gradually permeated by their ideological ambitions. All goods, wrote the magazine *Esprit* in one of its doctrine-defining issues, beyond those satisfying personal needs should be distributed among the community. This may become the ideal of a small group of equals; but in complex societies where productivity has immensely increased the amount of all holdings, public and private, the restriction of goods to the strictly needed amount puts in the hands of the community's manager, the State, a wealth out of all proportions to what it allots to the individual. It is no longer the question of a small group in which the common holding would be ten, twenty, fifty times as much as what each individual needs for his personal use, but of a modern society where the State would be many million times richer than any individual, consequently several million times more powerful too, or rather alone powerful.

No question that the terrain was slippery in the direction already indicated: first impatience, then disappointment. The third phase is a search for more understanding allies, and such are usually found among the similarly impatient ones who, however, are militants of the opposite camp and for whom impatience is part of their ideology. On April 24, 1933, Mounier quoted a Protestant magazine apropos of militant atheism in Soviet Russia: "Let us rejoice. Mankind has accumulated so much moral dirt that divine cleansing must perhaps begin by a total negation. Faith will not be torn from the heart of the persecuted. But afterwards they will be better prepared to meet Him!" A sinister text, yet Mounier comments only: It is the same for me too . . .[28] It was equally easy to slip from the plane of social justice to that of doctrinal reform. Mounier asked for the dismantling of various Catholic institutions whose field was the temporal world, because the Christian ought to work together with all other men in the City which belongs to all. In view of this action in common a new type of priest ought to be encouraged, not educated in seminaries, one who would no longer be a "separated man through the habit he wears and through his inactivity (sic), but would have a civil occupation."[29] This is already a call for the worker–priests (later condemned by Pius XII) and foreshadows the present clamor for the abolition of priesthood.

Thus, we see Mounier and his group turn increasingly to what Pius X described as the heresy of modernism, and so repeat the same errors which were evident in former times. One such error had been part of Ockham's theory of the State: the Empire (secular power) for which he fought against the papacy was not, in his view, a natural thing, but rather an institution through which God was punishing people and correcting their deficiencies caused by the fall.[30] Mounier's circle subscribed to this thesis. One of

them, the Russian writer, Berdyaev, who had joined their
ranks and became a Catholic, wrote that facing communism
the Christian society is cast in the culprit's role because it
had failed to live according to truth and has betrayed it.[31]
This is angelism again, the expectation of absolute purity,
short of which one deserves devilish punishment. Indeed, the
attraction of the "Soviet experience" became for the *Esprit*
group increasingly irresistible. They knew of its horrors as
the words of Berdyaev show, yet they were undecided between two attitudes. Was communism, in the divine order
of things, a chastisement for the sins of capitalism and the
bourgeoisie? or was it rather (*also*) something good in its
own right, a way of redistributing wealth, spreading more
social justice, abolishing the tsarist regime's cruelties? If
not quite the same thoughts as Bonhoeffer's, nevertheless
thoughts leading to similar conclusions and actions,—because it seemed to *Esprit* that history now handed over the
leadership role to communism,—as it seemed to Bonhoeffer
that God handed over his creation to man. In both cases
the issue is the waning of God's presence and providence
in the eyes of these Christians who, with all their worldly
enthusiasm, were really pesisimists from the Christian point
of view. But Christian pessissism turns into mundane opti-
mism—both for Bonhoeffer and Mounier—a faith transferred
from God to the world, more specifically to the "historical
force" which seems to dynamize and propel the world at
a given moment. In the 1930s and 1940s, this force was
communism. Mounier reports on a conversation (November
30, 1930) among five friends who were to be among the
founders of *Esprit,* with Maritain, oldest and most famous
of the group, participating. They debated the attitude the
group would take vis-a-vis the "Soviet fact" as they called
it. Maritain condemned the hostility of the western press
and was in favor of giving the Soviet regime "the maximum
understanding" (*sympathie*). After all, he argued, the new
regime made a general housecleaning in Russia. It represented a new worldview, "the most formidable effort to

date to eliminate God, and this is what makes the regime so tremendous. This is also the reason why one should not attempt to interfere from outside, but wait for the rebirth of the souls." Another member argued for prayers but otherwise a hands-off attitude so that the Russians "might now follow their freedom. Let us allow them to go to the depth of things; we shall see what the results of God's total absence will be."[32]

Not every member of this and other discussion groups showed himself so prayerfully heartless (if one may say), yet even these few quotations suffice to grasp the gist of the Christian humanist position as it has crystallized in the past half a century. The essence of this position was that God and his Church had historically failed; (Godless) man now takes matters in his hands, either because God is powerless or with his approval, but anyway because God abdicated. The Christian, because *he* cannot abdicate and must work for the fulfillment of the promise (*what* promise if God has resigned?), should cooperate with the new man, builder of a better world. Today, the builder is a regime, an ideology, admittedly hostile to Christianity, but one never knows how it may turn out. As Maritain noted in the course of the discussion, the saints too are revolutionary! He did not ask himself whether it follows that revolutionaries are saints. Thus, the only difference one may finally detect between the attitudes of Bonhoeffer and the *Esprit* group is that the first perceived the definitive absence of God from what follows now in history, in fact the illusoriness of God and Christianity in the past also—whereas the second did not exclude God's mysterious work in the background of history, but interpreted that work as temporarily favoring the secular cause. The nuance between the two positions follows from the difference between the Protestant notion that God is *totaliter aliter* and the Catholic notion that ultimately history has a divine meaning. In practice, however, the two positions are hardly distinguishable, since their origin is found in the impact that the power of secular events (rise of science, rise of secular civilization, rise of the totalitarian State) has had on disheartened Christians. The fascination with the manifestation of secular power splits their loyalty and risks turning their expectations towards the promise of the worldly kingdom. This is evident from Jarrett-Kerr's view: "The Christian, knowing that he is in a minority, should give every support to even those movements which by their success seem to disprove the Christian's case."[33] If this applies to today's conditions, why not also to conditions in the Roman Empire when the Christian sect was a minority and was mocked, persecuted, and martyrized? So much self-flagellation and masochism cannot be taken as a serious proposal. True, the above quoted *Letter to Diognetes* encouraged all Christians to do their duty vis-a-vis (pagan) society and State, but this means not at all a surrender to its spirit, but merely the recognition of the legitimacy of society and State, as argued by St. Paul. Precisely this recognition dictates to the Christian, the duty to permeate society and state with the spirit of Christianity— and not to allow them to fall victim to Godless powers and laws. If interpreted in today's terms, the message to Diognetes does not imply for Christians to join the Communist party. It is not Christianity but Gnosticism for which everything wordly is contemptible because of being created by Satan, which despises State and society, and preaches total withdrawal from them. Jarrett-Kerr's suggestion is, contrary to appearances, not an encouragement for the Christian to participate in bettering the world, it subtly implies that the Christian *qua* Christian has nothing to contribute.

Maritain himself was probably the leading figure, at least in the first half of the century, of Christian humanism. His works, primarily the famous and influential *Integral Humanism* (1936) constitute a grandiose attempt to clear a path in the jungle of ideologies: capitalism, liberalism, Marxism, and various humanisms, and formulate a new humanism, theocentric in its fundamental orientation, yet satisfying modern man's expectations from his secularized environment. To speak in terms of praise of Maritain's work is not to find it flawless since, understandably after quoting his interventions in the *Esprit* debates, one cannot agree with some of the basic elements of his position. His is merely the merit of having traveled the length and width of the Christian humanist area of discourse, a travel which includes a venture to the borders of this area where it is risky for a Catholic to tread. Also in Maritain's case we have the rare opportunity of observing the Christian humanist position as it evolved in the same mind in the course of thirty years. It was indeed in 1966 that Maritain, by then withdrawn from active life to a monastery, published *Le Paysan de la Garonne,* a new and last summation of, among other things, his social-political philosophy, read eagerly by his many disciples and critics who wanted to see if the author would confirm or reject his earlier views.

Maritain's position in *Integral Humanism* was, generally, that the Christian must engage in political action so as to counteract all forms of totalitarianism, and to liquidate as well the other anthropocentric alternative, bourgeois capitalism. "The new political formations should be conceived as temporal fellowships . . . acting as ferments . . . (and arise) from the midst of proletarian elites collaborating with intellectuals."[34] The alternative to this Catholic action is martyrdom at the hands of totalitarian regimes, a choice Thomas More would not rule out, but only after attempting to employ all the means at his disposal to escape from the alternative. Such means today, Maritain wrote, are political groupings, a Catholic press, and the various education- and action-oriented, Church sponsored organizations of youth, workers, actors, students, and so on. These proposals were not isolated instances; similar calls were heard at the same time from Simone Weil, Dom Sturzo, and a number of prelates, for example, Cardinal Gerlier. As said before, the echo was particularly enthusiastic in South America where the problems of a capitalist society had just begun to appear and where positivism had ruled the universities for a century.

One cannot say that Maritain did not consider all sides of the issue already in 1936 and did not warn against the separation of spiritual and temporal. Artistic, social, and political activity must be turned toward God as its final end, but has as its direct determining aim goods which concern the things of time, civilization, or culture. He denounced the separation of the two planes as it had been attempted only too often by Machiavelli, by the Protestant Reformation, by Descartes. He made the same points in 1966: "The Christian must want the coming of God's kingdom in glory—but he must not propose as the goal of history's and of his own temporal activity the final coming of justice and peace, and of human happiness. This kind of progress cannot find its end here below."[35] The trouble is that the relatively subtle distinctions Maritain made between spiritual and temporal were not sufficiently understood in the feverish climate of this century. On the preceding pages we have pointed out several times that the Christian tension is difficult to live with and that the temptation is always renewed to find immortality and salvation integrated with earthly existence. This does not mean that a Christian humanism is a contradictory, let alone an evil enterprise; but it may be admitted that it contains seeds of contradiction which at times represent an unbearable stress for those who accept the burden. One can look at what happened to various Catholic action groups in France: Jeunesse Ouvière Catholique, Jeunesse Etudiante Catholique, also to the various periodicals welcomed by Maritain, among them *Esprit*—to realize that the weight of Marxist ideology finally pulled down to itself the Catholic initiative.

Moreover, in a sense the tragedy of Christian humanism itself is demonstrated in Maritain's own case. His lucid analyses of philosophical Marxism are models of criticism; yet he is not excempt from the belief that, after all, communism would not have been so successful without the

Christian and capitalist errors committed by Christians and capitalists. Two observations must be made in response to the Maritainian position. Man in history is not wiser than in his private life; imperfection is the rule on both planes. Does he therefore deserve punishment? In a sense, he does, although this view reminds one of the Greek concept of *hybris* which brings automatic vengeance by the gods. But in another sense, even if this punishment is deserved, it is a tragedy because it is not meant as an occasion to learn and improve.[36] We may say that communism did not step into a criminally neglected vacuum, as a rectifier of historical errors and mismangement, it is principally, as Marx admitted it, a systematic effort at the abolition of God so as to establish a materialist society. It is not less materialist than capitalism, and it excludes transcendence, unlike Christianity. Thus, it is difficult to see in what sense does communism represent a "punishment," let alone an improvement.

The second observation is that Maritain fell victim to a fashionable dichotomy which judges two species of totalitarianism with an unequal measure. He regarded fascism as being without any saving grace, whereas communism, in spite of its horrors and atheistic militancy, as a kind of vehicle for social verities, valid in themselves, although properly belonging to the Christian sphere of action. Thus, Maritain himself opened the door to further excesses by Christian "progressives" who have gone as far as to regard Maoism as "expressing the essence of Christianity" (Louvain Seminar, summer 1974) and to recommend Chou Enlai for canonization (Archbishop Mendez Arceo, of Cuernavaca).

What is pointed out here is not that Maritain indulged in such recklessness. In fact, *The Peasant of the Garonne* abounds in ironic remarks about the grotesque "kneeling before the world" of prelates, priests, and Catholic intellectuals. The book begins with the statement that compared to the neo–modernism of the present (Conciliar period and after), the modernism condemned by Pius X in 1910 appears like a mild hay-fever.[37] Yet, Maritain's case is illustrative of Christian humanism beyond the forms it has assumed in our time; it instructs us about the very substance of Christian humanism. Maritain's and his friends' fascination with Marxism is similar, thus typical, to previous attitudes: Pico's before Renaissance man's unlimited potentialities, Descartes' before the unlimited power of science, Teilhard de Chardin's before the irresistible sweep of evolution, etc. But let us remember that Maritain was impressed not only by Marxism, but also, later, by American democracy. One may even wonder if what Louis Salleron calls Maritain's "democratic faith"[38] is not the deepest root also of his earlier tenderness toward communism. This democratic faith is not a specific admiration for the way democracy organizes the citizen's life, it is rather an expression of the belief that history is a substance, facing God, another substance. And while Maritain spent great efforts to resubordinate the first to the second, he cannot hide, cannot give up, his humanist fascination with the turns and tricks of history. Impressed first by Marxism, then by Americanism, he is really impressed by the power of the secular component, although theoretically and as a Catholic philosopher, he is committed to the divine component. As we saw, this is not rare, it is indeed typical of the Christian humanists' spiritual-intellectual make-up. If Maritain finally abandoned his attraction to communism, it is because "the communist revolution has lost its historic steam . . . and the creative energy of history has shifted to new history-making events."[39] What are they and where are they supposed to be found? "If there is any hope for the sprouting of a new Christiandom in the modern world, it is in America that the historical and ethico-social ground which could become a soil for such a sprouting may be found."[40] Pascal said of Descartes that he kept God as a force setting the world into motion, but then no longer needed him; analogically, we might say that Maritain evokes God as the guarantor of man's spiritual dimension, but has no use for him once he, Maritain, has the privilege of watching, fascinated, the working of history. It is not God and not history that switched from Russia to America, from Marxism to Americanism, it is Maritain himself who sought to guess in advance "the temporal eschatologies so as to attune each in turn to his Christian eschatology."[41]

We possess now enough historical and contemporary material about christian humanism to attempt an overview and some reflection about it. No question that the Christian religion furnished the humanist movement with its essential anxiety and restlessness as it becomes manifest from the conflict, already alive at the Renaissance, between Christians who were humanists (Colet, More, Marsilius Ficinus, Erasmus) and humanists still working within the Christian credal orbit. It was the Christian ingredient which supplied the background for Pico della Mirandola when he spoke of man's unfinished creation, his self-choice, his quasi–infinite growth and potential. But while the Christian elements persisted in humanism almost up to the threshold of the contemporary world, the real split occurred between the two humanisms when the secular spirit, until then rebellious and defiant only, became embodied in institutions, political parties, ideological movements, and even the State—in other words, acquired political power. The new phenomenon with which Christian humanists had to come to terms was a rival church to theirs, one increasingly powerful and occupying man's entire attention. At the same time Christianity became increasingly marginal, or at least it was perceived as such: in science, social issues, the political good, the ideological liberation.

The loss of public authority by the Church and the gains of the same authority by the secular world favored the cause of Christian Humanism. We said that the term "humanism" is no longer quite correct, if it is read in the Renaissance context; it is nevertheless characteristic that it is in continuous use, as shown by the title of Maritain's book. But even if purists of the history of ideas might wish to coin a new word, it remains that "humanism" expresses correctly one pole of the Christian tension.[42] A tension entails a risk, in fact two risks, two potential excesses. In this case, to deny the human, or to deny the divine. The temptation and the risk were obviously *wanted* by man's creator, but in a way different from the temptation of evil which He *permitted* (see the story of Job). Adam had been appointed *before* the sin to be a steward of nature; we may interpret this as also "keeper of his brother." It was *after* the sin that evil became habitually tempting, and, alas, less than habitually resisted. The root of humanism—to be one's brother's keeper—is thus not rooted in sin, it flows from man's ante-peccatum nature. This still allows for a "bad humanism," but also for a good and generous one. The first has become particularly blatant in modern times: It is the Christian's submission to and cooperation with the essence of secularism. The second has always been evident in the grasp of man as both divine and human. Thus, to be working for the truly human community is *not* to work for secularism; Christian humanism is a legitimate enterprise.

The limit, as in most cases human, is hard to find and perhaps impossible to define. All we can do is explore the limit situations on both sides. Where does each lead?

First, *Christian secularism*—which we distinguished already earlier from Christian humanism—arises from the fact that "man is a being with possibility, hence, anxiety,"[43] so that he searches for the land of certitudes, utopia. The apparent ambiguity of incarnation (ambiguity because it elevated man, yet left the human condition outwardly intact) exacerbated the anxiety by accelerating the sense of urgency for conditions worthy of man's elevated status. For some, God's new nearness suffices as an exalting plenitude; in the eyes of others, the impatient ones, the Gospels preached the earthly kingdom, or at least prompted the establishment of an earthly mirror-image of the divine beatitude. This would be the ideal society, an expression in which the word "ideal" does not so much signify good, pleasant, comfortable, harmonious, peaceful, but rather the elimination of man's divided nature, the abolition of the tension entailed in theocentrism. This is why the zealots of utopia usually end up with a blueprint where the divine is absorbed by the earthly authority (State, State-church, immanent priesthood, World Council, etc.) and the burden of "dual citizenship" is lifted from the inhabitants' shoulders.

We find today a growing and spreading situation of secularist-utopian design, either proclaiming the "death of God," a crude quasiphilosophical endeavor, or, even more popular, the revolutionary nature of Jesus and his enterprise. One might say that the secularists, and among them Christians with lost hopes are numerous, have found in this their trump-card, that they pinned all their secularist hopes on this one issue. If Jesus was a revolutionary, then not only is revolution the center piece of history, at the same time the divine action resolves itself in human action, man is vindicated as creator of his own destiny and history. One might say that some great Christian scholars unwittingly contribute to this interpretation of Jesus's mission. Thus, the Protestant theologian, Oscar Cullmann, opines that Jesus was not aware that time would continue long after his earthly course, so that he only demanded the conversion of hearts, without concerning himself with a reform of social structures.[44] But it stands to reason that any knower of men is aware that structural reforms, no matter how hard to carry out, are still infinitely easier than the *metanoia* of the human heart, the turn from evil to good that Jesus preached. Truth is, Jesus was not a "Hebrew patriot" (nor were the prophets purely that), a sympathizer with the radicals against the presence of the Roman occupant, nor a social revolutionary of the agrarian reformer or of any other type. He knew that parousia was not for the next day and also that his "good news" was not the proclamation of social reforms. One proof is that none of the apostles or other hearers of his message turned his words to "social" uses in the revolutionary sense, although it is notorious that disciples and epigones simplify and vulgarize their master's teaching, as it is also notorious that the message was fastest spread among lower classes and slaves, still with no social overtones. Outside of a few so-called "Judaizing" Christians, with Peter leaning to their side but not among them, who, quite naturally, wanted to remain loyal to Jewish law, we hear nothing of a "socialist" branch or sect of Jesus's followers. This is significant because in the overheated atmosphere of the Palestine between A.D. 30 and A.D. 70 (from Jesus' mission to the destruction of Jerusalem by Titus) reports would have reached us if Christ's movement had been understood in a revolutionary sense. On the contrary, alerted by the master's predictions about the fate of the capital, the Christian community had left the city long before the military actions started.

Cullmann himself draws a moderate conclusion from his thesis. Christians may collaborate with such secular groups whose ideals are "close to the Gospels," and the condition of the collaboration is the Christians' freedom to speak as Christians, not just repeating the group's own language. "In their [the non-Christians'] interest he must have the courage to oppose a categorical No, if the ends and means employed contradict the Gospels."[45] This suggestion is indeed useful as an indication of the limit of which we spoke earlier, even though in concrete situations the onus of interpretation remains heavy. Such concrete situations abound today, and we shall look only at the farthest.

The desire to regain the world for Christianity, namely what is called the world of the "social issue," of the working class, has prompted Christian humanism from Lamennais to Maritain to deepen the exploration of historical (immanent) eschatologies. Since it was not a church-guided exploration but pursued in the growing shadow of a parallel and increasingly powerful secular exploration, it ended in the modernism anathemized by Pius X, then, with a second impetus, in the work of Maritain and beyond. By that time, however, the logic of secularism had reached rock bottom in the first absolutely secular State, Soviet Russia. We saw the reaction of the *Esprit* group to this phenomenon, a reaction of mixed impotence, curiosity, expectation, and prayer. Also a wish to "catch up," to selectively imitate, to baptize. Similar developments had occurred in the Protestant area somewhat earlier because they were unchecked by a magisterium, so everybody could follow his own inspiration. As Paul Tillich reminds us, in the late nineteenth century various ministers were stressing the freedom of God to act apart from the church "as a sociological entity."[46] Some of them became leaders of socialist movements, this being consistent with their conviction that God loved the world, not only the Church and not only Christians. Christoph Blumhardt, who died in 1919, sounded like many post-Vatican II Catholic theologians when he argued that the works of atheists are often more God-centered than the work done in the Church by Christians. Tillich himself describes the ecumenical meeting called the Oxford Conference (1937) at which it was decided that through revolutionary movements like socialism and communism God speaks often more directly than inside the churches. It is then easy to understand that the sociological analysis of bourgeois social structure was increasingly performed in Marxist terms and with Marxism as the one competent science. The only Christian elements in these analyses were names given to the condemned structures: They were called manifestations of the "demonic," and the Marxist break into the complacent temporal order received the name "kairos," the right time.[47]

At the end of the era of religious socialism in Germany and of Maritainian Christian humanism in France and generally in Latin countries (the two had a combined and powerful impact on Christians in the United States, mostly through the presence of Jacques Maritain and Paul Tillich on American soil), we find the Christian religion practically disarmed vis-a-vis the secular power of State and society. In one respect, it is like a stream of water slowly absorbed by the all-surrounding sand; thus, we see Christians, both Catholic and Protestant, voting for laws approving abortion. By so doing, they do not perhaps give their inner assent to immorality, but, exhausted in the battle against total and ubiquitous secularization, they choose the ambiguous language of Christian humanism as a soothing potion for their conscience. In sum, they have surrendered to the dialectics which shows them the inevitability of the secular world's victory, and they comfort themselves with the belief that the secular world, being democratic, tolerant, and pluralistic, has at least integrated a certain number of Christian ideals. Though more nuanced, this was also Maritain's position.

Such notions are less easy to entertain when Christians face the secular leviathan itself, the totalitarian State. By then, the Christian stream fighting the sand of secularization is not even a trickle, and of the four reactions I listed above as those of *Esprit* in the 1930s only one, prayer, remains as practicable. This is also the overall response of religious authorities to the issue of *Christians under communism*. It is then interesting to examine this end of the line because it also serves as a conclusion to the Christian humanist argumentation. What shall the Christian do when the issue of social justice is monopolized by the secular State which calls this monopoly "final solution"? And the monopoly implies just that: No one else is permitted to think it further because, by definition, there are no problems after Marxist man has solved all of them.

This issue would not be one if the framework for the alleged solution—the communist State with Christian citizens—had been only forcibly imposed, without any sort of cooperation from the Christian side. There would be then no crisis of conscience. Fact is, Christian humanists in large numbers had as little understanding of Marxism as they or their fathers had had of other secularist doctrines. When they found themselves in the communist State, the already well-known dilemma presented itself to them: to what extent did history not just bring about, but actually *justify* such a State—namely as God's punishment for Christian sins, as a self-sustained secular promise, as the natural crowning of the Gospels? In other words, the nature of Christian humanist reasoning did not change; only under the label of Christian democracy or Christian socialism it now entered, in West and East, the political realm in the shape it always hoped it would: as one among the many options that the democratic political system, itself an outgrowth of Christianity, suddenly offered.[48]

The Secular City now exists and it is unmistakably the Other Church. It presents to people generally, among them the Christians, those "concrete proposals" which, Karl Rahner wrote, were more needed today than the "useless talk of Christian principles of salvation." Thus, from the safety of the outside world, the noncommunist world, the fascination with History and its allegedly irresistible product, the Secular State, did not cease. From inside, things look differently, but, after all, this could have been foreseen. We may usefully turn to a brief outline of the Church's position in communist countries where Christian civilization is a thousand years old. We learn from it not only about how the Christian tension is solved, but also why the Christian secularist is still attracted by the model. We shall not go into details, but content ourselves with some indications.

Although reduced to a skeletal state, the Church's formal structure still exists.[49] There are bishops, priests, (State-supervised) catechism classes, and mass is celebrated. A few seminarians are every year authorized to pursue their studies, but no religious orders and no religious schools are tolerated. The clergy is also only a skeleton of its earlier self: The believers never know whether the sermon, dealing with social and political issues, is imposed or represents the priest's real views, since he may be only a so-called "peace priest" or State functionary. The bishops whom the government recommends to Rome for consecration are carefully selected among the weaker characters who had compromised themselves either in their moral life or through their excessive subservience to the regime. In one word, Lenin's strategy prevails: no frontal attack against the church, but a slow process of reducing it to irrelevance as a tolerated remnant of a once forceful historical body. A position rather like that of the *haruspices* (bird watchers) in imperial Rome's priesthood of whom it was said that they laughed upon seeing one another.

With the sacerdotal functions reduced to a minimum, and even those operating under steady control, what are the policies of Christian churches? They can be summed up in two points: The church accepts the historical changes and also partnership with the State. We see at once why Christian secularists approve it: If profane history grows on a parallel course with sacred history, then it is now the former's turn—the State's over the Church's—to lead mankind. This leadership is admittedly harsh, but the Christians' previous sins were also crying to heaven. A kind of justice is restored, and whether God wanted it this way or he wanted only his own withdrawal, the new historical Absolute is legitimate. The second basic point is partnership with the State. Not an assent to official atheism, as the bishops keep pointing out, yet a loyal cooperation. As Bishop Joseph Cserhati of Pecs (Hungary) wrote in a manifesto (1975), the church is present in the shaping of the communal spirit on the moral level, it combats crime and preaches against selfishness. These are vague words but they can be fitted into Fr. Häring's recommendations that the church's mission is to participate in the world and to be active in the world's life. In other terms, to be active the way the world is active, without any specific difference suggested. This is only a parody of the *Letter to Diognetes* where the Christian was told that he is *in* but not *of* the world, and that his whole justification for acting in the world is derived precisely from his not being of the world. But this teaching finds no place in the neopagan State since the whole point of the secular city and of the

Christian secularists is that what used to be "two worlds" for St. Augustine, now form only one. It is the *civitas terrena,* but no longer the "bandits' den" of Augustine's description since social justice is now by definition an accomplished fact, a department jealously claimed by the secular State.

The secular State is not necessarily approved entirely by the Christian secularists, it is regarded, nonetheless, as a new, original, and progressive form, at any rate a new point of departure for something in the same order but still better. Yet this "better" does not have to mean a larger freedom for Catholics, and certainly not for their Church. Ockham's old and insufficiently grasped ideal has, after all, come true: The secular power dominates the spiritual one, even though Ockham could not foresee [?] what exactly this might mean. On this point, the communist State's ecclesiastical policy by and large satisfies the Christian secularist. Where he would press for reform is, strangely, more secularization in the sense of more political freedom of option for the citizen, but a freedom exercised only for secular purposes (democratization), not for the strengthening of the ecclesiastical structures. This policy is not substantially different from that of the Freemasons under communist regimes. Rare is the Christian secularist who would want to strengthen religion in the Secular state other than an amorphous spirituality issuing in a deeper commitment to social justice, the latter by now devoid of meaning. The Marsilian ambition of quasidismantling the ecclesiastical structures remains strong in the Christian secularist view. Although it would be useful to counter the secular State and its tremendous power with a similarly strong ecclesiastical structure—as seems to be the case in Poland, for example, where the Church· is still able to protect the citizen from the Party's power.

Let us explore now the second limit situation of Christian humanism. "The World," writes T. S. Eliot, "is trying the experiment of attempting to form a civilized but non-Christian mentality. The experiment will fail but we must be very patient in awaiting its collapse, meanwhile redeeming the time.''[50] This might sum up the present Christian reaction to the dead-end street of Christian humanism with its exaggerated sense of urgency. Once again, it should be stated that the modern world did not come into existence through the travails and agonies of Christian humanism, the latter accompanied only the modern world's birth and development with an increased feeling of anguish lest this world becomes completely alienated from Christianity. But it is no less certain that Christian humanists since Lamennais regarded themselves as the marching wing of the Church, the only bridge between Christianity and the modern world. In this sense they share some of the responsibility for the turn of the modern world in the direction of the secular State and society—a turn that the Christian humanists promoted rather than hindered.

But is the patience recommended by Eliot an adequate, a sufficient response? Our answer would risk becoming a treatise on political philosophy, unless we consider, and keep within the limits of, the relative narrowness of our subject, Christian humanism. The question thus amounts to asking whether Christian humanism itself is redeemable, whether the built-in temptation for Christians to stress the *man* in the incarnate Christ may be resisted within the Christian humanist area of discourse? In short, is there a more authentic, more balanced humanism for Christians than the one whose failure we are witnessing?

Fr. Montcheuil answered this question when he chose the term *apostolate,* without, be it understood, repudiating the expression "Christian humanism." The true desire of the apostolate, he wrote, finds its source in the sacraments which incorporate us to the Church and make us live from them ever more fully.[51] This thought is inseparable in our context from one already quoted where Montcheuil enjoins the Christian to remain detached and free from any and all institution to the establishment of which he may have contributed. At first, this sounds like a harsh as well as unrealistic demand: Is it human to bring one's zeal to an accomplishment, then become aloof from it? Yet, this seems to be the lesson of the times, indeed of all times: prudence in one's involvement (*engagement*) and a constant return to the sacramental sources for inspiration and wisdom.

This is not timidity in the face of action; it is refusal to enter the kind of action that today is considered under the label of "revolution," "mutation," "the new man," "the believer's adulthood," and so on. The danger is at once obvious when we realize that these labels hide, by their nature, rival religions since as soon as they appear there spouts within them a new theology, the "theology of revolution," the "theology of the death of God," or Teilhard's system who wished to "graft the new Catholicism on the old Roman stem," but was ready to jettison the latter if Rome did not consent to the hybridization. Even when the attempt is less radical than in the foregoing cases, it hardly escapes becoming an anti-Christian position. Take, for example, Karl Rahner's statement: "A new active entity is forced into existence. It can only be the State or the community of peoples organized at a planetary level . . . in which the Catholics must accept a diaspora situation." Strictly speaking, there is no doctrinal error in this sentence, as there was, strictly speaking, no doctrinal error in Pico's and Descartes's systems either. Pascal's genius was needed to point out the source of wrongness in the latter, the shelving of God as a continuous creator.[52] Rahner's system also shelves God; things happen because History wills them. In Rahner's case the inspiration follows Heidegger's philosophy, perhaps the most consistent and thorough-going atheism of our time. "For Heidegger," Paul Tillich wrote, "utopia is the revelation of pure being which he awaits like a prophet who gazes upon a holy mountain. . . . Should this revelation come, the age of metaphysics would be at an end, that is the age in which man attaches himself to the forms of being instead of to pure being. . . . This hidden utopia of the existentialists shows how even the radical extrahistorical form of thinking eventually finds its lot bound up with history."[53]

Rahner's planetary State is the mundane version of pure being. One does not have to use the revolutionary label and drink from purely secular sources to engage in some form of non-Christian systematization, hence, non-Christian action. Utopian thinking is nearest to heretical systems[54] and the revolutionary labels mentioned earlier carry in themselves the seeds of utopia, the purely political organization in which God is discarded and replaced by man's handiwork.

It is then not from *action* that the Christian ought to abstain, it is from the systematization of action according to an alien, non-Christian mode of thought. Christianity was always a religion of action; what else did Paul, Ambrose, Augustine, Benedict do but vigorously knead the human material; what else did the baptizers of tribes and nations do, or the Christian kings, the builders of cathedrals, the conceivers of universities, the founders of orders, the organizers of hospitals, the ralliers of charity, up to the twentieth-century missionaries? Theocentric man is also an action man, the difference between him and an activist is that he acts for God and that this permeates his work with prudence, patience, and charity. His action is concrete, directed to the here-and-now, and does not sacrifice generations for a hypothetical shiny future, does not sacrifice this concrete man here for the hypothetical masses of tomorow. Only concrete action for real human beings resembles God's action in eternity. Other kinds of actions are often mere idolatrous rites on the altar of time.

Is what I describe here Christian *humanism?* The expression may appear like a pleonasm, since the first word contains the second. Yet, the term humanism also has its use. Rightly understood, it can mean that the tension of incarnation is unavoidable, it must be lived as long as there are men on this earth. Unless we believe that the secular age upon which we have entered and the coryphees of which never cease mocking the theocentric man, is the final chapter of history—unless we believe this we must continue being "humanists," that is "friends of man," the way the *Letter to Diognetes* teaches.

Footnotes to Chapter Two

1. *God and Philosophy,* Yale University Press, 1941, 1969, p. 56.

2. "The Meaning of 'God Speaks,'" *The New Scholasticism,* Spring 1969.

3. *Catholicisme,* Coll. Foi vivante, Ed. du Cerf, 1965, p. 152.

4. *Problèmes de vie spirituelle,* Ed. de l'Epi, 1963, p. 156.

5. *Freedom in the Modern World,* pp. 89/90.

6. Oscar Cullmann, *Études de Théologie biblique,* ("Etudes sur l'histoire et l'histoire du salut"), Delachaux & Niestlé, Neuchâtel/Paris, 1968, p. 123.

7. Cf. Georges de Lagarde, *La Naissance de l'esprit laique,* vols. I-V, ed. B. Nauwelaerts, Louvain.

8. *The Origins of the Great Schism,* 1948, p. 184.

9. *Les Origines des sciences humaines,* quoted in H. de Lubac, *Pic de la Mirandole,* Aubier-Montaigne, 1974, p. 120.

10. In the *Heptaplus,* quoted in H. de Lubac, *op. cit.,* p. 82.

11. *Théologie de l'histoire,* Ed. du Seuil, 1968, p. 79.

12. Quoted in Lucien Febvre, *Le Problème de l'incroyance au 16e siècle,* Ed. Albin Michel, 1962, p. 133.

13. Busson, *Le Rationalisme dans la littérature française de la Renaissance,* Librarie philosophique J. Vrin, 1957, p. 114.

14. This total freedom led soon, however, to a cruel repression of any noncomformist belief or act. In 1524, in *Against the Celes-*

tial Prophets, that is those who took Luther's encouragement literally and began founding sects, Luther fulminates: "The only way of making Herr Omnes (Mr. everybody) do what he must is to compel him by the law and by the sword, the way one holds wild beasts chained in a cage." Calvin had similar troubles —and reactions. (Cf. Busson, *ibid,* 318/9).

15. E. Gilson, "Calvinisme et Philosophie," *Itinéraires,* mai 1967, p. 35.

16. In this it succumbed unwittingly to the Protestant challenge. For it is the protestant thesis that philosophy cannot speak of God, only of mundane matters. Of God only God can speak (the "word of God"), this is neither theology nor human wisdom. And since reason is corrupt and ignorant, philosophy must focus on worldly matters. Hence, from Descartes on, philosophy turns into a reflection of science and the verifiable world of matter and mind.

17. *God and Philosophy,* p. 89.

18. *Integral Humanism,* Ch. Scribner's Sons, 1968, pp. 19-20.

19. *Ibid.,* p. 205.

20. *Ibid.,* p. 199.

21. So as not to create confusion, I shall continue to refer to "Christian humanism," although the term "Christian secularism" would be more expressive of the phenomenon, and will be used in the appropriate context.

22. *Théologie de l'histoire,* p. 155.

23. *Encyclopedia.* My italics call attention to the Protestant concept of God as absolutely other. While for Catholics too God and man are completely distinct, the personal God in his mercy, charity, and providence is not severe, distant, and arbitrarily selective. (Cf. Thomas Molnar, *God and the Knowledge of Reality,* Basic Books, 1973).

24. *The Secular Promise,* SCM Press, London, 1964, pp. 26-7.

25. *Mounier et sa génération,* ed. du Seuil, 1956, p. 150. Mounier's italics.

26. *Ibid.*, p. 180.

27. B. Jaye Miller, "Anarchism and French Catholicism in *Esprit*," *Journal of the History of Ideas*, vol. XXXVII/1, Jan-March 1976, p. 169.

28. *Mounier et sa génération*, p. 122.

29. *Ibid.*, p. 261.

30. G. de Lagarde, *op. cit.*, vol. V, p. 311. Later, this was to be also Calvin's view.

31. Quoted in Maritain, *Freedom in the Modern World*, p. 121.

32. *Mounier et sa génération*, p. 66.

33. *Ibid.*, p. 184.

34. *Integral Humanism*, pp. 272-3.

35. *Le Paysan de la Garonne*, Desclée de Brouwer, 1966, p. 294.

36. I remember a conversation in Brazil with Archbishop Dom Helder Camara who told me that the Hungarian Church deserved the communist whip for her historical alliance with the feudal system!

37. *Ibid.*, p. 16.

38. "Une philosophie de l'histoire," *La Nation Française*, dec. 1959.

39. *On the Philosophy of History*, Ch. Scribner's Sons, 1957, p. 68.

40. *Ibid.*, p. 161.

41. Louis Salleron, *loc. cit.*

42. Meanwhile let us bear in mind that "humanitas" as a literary focus came into existence as a term set off from "divinitas," the focus of medieval studies.

43. Paul Tillich, *Political Expectations*, p. 140.

44. *Jésus et les révolutionnaires de son temps*, Delachaux & Niestlé, 1970, p. 75.

45. *Ibid.*, p. 79.

46. *A History of Christian Thought,* Simon and Schuster, 1967, p. 531.

47. *Ibid.*, pp. 533-4.

48. This was particularly clear in Chile where the Christian-democrats of Ed. Frei (a specially honored friend of Maritain) voted in large numbers for the Marxist candidate, Salvador Allende, in the 1970 presidential elections. In Chile no foreign army imposed the Marxist rule on the Christian democrats; indeed, they could have blocked Allende's election as the strongest party, forcing a rerun between Allende and the nationalist candidate, Alessandri. For two years afterwards, the Christian-democrats found themselves in a similar situation as other Christian-democratic parties in Eastern Europe. In the end, it was not they, but the army which put an end to the Marxist regime.

49. What follows is based on facts, but these facts are not the same in every communist country. In Poland and Yugoslavia the situation is more encouraging; in Cuba, Russia and China it is infinitely worse. I took the average situation, without naming any country.

50. "Thoughts after Lambeth," in *Selected Essays,* 1931.

51. Montcheuil, *Ibid.*, p. 62.

52. Malebranche, Descartes's disciple, tried to remedy Descartes' neglect but in a very clumsy manner.

53. *Political Expectations,* p. 146.

54. Cf. my *Utopia, the Perennial Heresy,* Sheed & Ward, 1967.

CHAPTER

3.

Religion and Humanism

The impression the reader may derive from the first two chapters of this work is that humanism has too many facets to be an easily identifiable and manageable concept, and that the label has been applied to a number of doctrines proposed inside and outside the Church. After all, movements like Joachitism and individual theories like those of the Cardinal of Cusa cannot be called, strictly speaking, "humanistic," nor can they be said to have been entirely unorthodox. Our answer is that it would be hard to limit humanism to only those who coined the term and accepted it as their own description. Proof is that Fr. de Lubac chose, as the title of his celebrated book, the drama of *atheistic humanism,* knowing perfectly well that Feuerbach, Comte, and Nietzsche who form his topic did not even remotely apply the humanist label to themselves, and that no history of Western thought in the nineteenth century refers to them as humanists. Furthermore, while it is a fact that Joachim's doctrine of the eternal gospel and the *tertius status* (third age) was disapproved, although not officially condemned, by the Church, and that Cusanus had many critics in his lifetime and later, there has always been a considerable latitude in the Church for teachings vastly different among themselves, hence in some cases contrary to orthodoxy.

Yet, even without reference to De Lubac's uncontested authority on the subject, it is easy to show that the best method to deal with humanism in its relationship to the Christian religion is to take its wide definition as we have done it on these pages. Humanism then appears as one doctrinal movement under many labels, having in common

(a) the pulling down of transcendence to the plane of immanence; consequently

(b) the interpretation of the *civitas Dei* as a potential *civitas terrena;* and

(c) the glorification of man as a potentially absolute being, implicitly in no need of God.

All the other humanistic propositions can be derived from these three postulates.

Many in the Church are aware that, when everything is said, Humanism remains the great modern opponent of Christianity. As I am writing, there is in front of me the announcement of a mid-April 1977 colloquium of "prelates, theologians, social scientists, and political activists" (a revealing amalgam!) on humanism, scheduled to take place in St. Louis. I quote from the introductory paragraph, then a sample of the topics, in order to illustrate the centrality of their concern. "The purpose of the colloquium is to give Americans an in-depth and many-faceted opportunity to examine the Church's *historic* and *current* involvement in humanistic enterprises. . . . The *secularization* of what once was the Church's special visible and corporate witness in humanitarian works will be a key concern. . ." The participants are scheduled to address themselves to topics such as the future, the feminist movement, ministry in the world, religion as the basis of culture, revolution, the sociology of priesthood, Christian humanism, and others.[1] Now this may be an all-too wide variety of subjects for a three day meeting, which, by its nature, is not likely to deepen any of them; I mentioned it only to show how many concerns may be found under the humanist label, a perhaps surprising number in the eyes of those who would wish to reserve the term "humanism" to a particular enterprise in erudition at the time of the Renaissance.

But it is not only a question of peaceful debate over the various meanings of Humanism and the historic connection between it and Christianity. The present thrust of the new theology, analysed toward the end of Chapter One, is its future-orientedness which, however, has less to do with life in view of the Last Judgment, than with the rejection of the past, in other words of Church, tradition, the magisterium from Christ to Vatican II. As Paul VI said (January 7, 1970), "many can absolutely not tolerate the Church's 'yesterday.' All that is marked by the past—people, institutions, way of life, doctrines—is simply discarded. The critical spirit of the frenzied innovators condemns the whole ecclesiastical 'system' . . . in which they see only errors and mistakes, inability and blunders. If nothing happens to moderate this trend, we must envisage the hypothesis of a Church totally different from ours. There is talk of a Church for the new times where all ties of obedience, all limitations of personal freedom, as also all forms with a sacred character would be abolished."

The innovators's "frenzy," as the Pope calls it, is fueled, from two sources:

(a) the misinterpretation of the Christian religion which emerges periodically in different forms and may lead, in the Pope's words, to a "Church totally different from ours";

(b) the eagerness to seize upon the fashionable secular philosophies at hand with which to form a hybrid doctrine.

The result is an immanentist ideology to which the Christian cooperator lends his own religious fervor. Thus, while a colloquium in St. Louis registers the impact of Christian humanism on Church and society, in Paris the *Centre Jean-Bart* run by progressivist priests with the Cardinal's approval is engaged in grafting a vague Catholic terminology, partly borrowed from Joachim, the twelfth century abbot, on the positivistic doctrine of Auguste Comte. According to the particular ideology of this religious study center, we are now leaving behind the "first age of metaphysics, substances, and onto-theology" in which the faithful were obedient to the Church, itself tied to "Western values"; and we are entering, after today's short intermediate period,[2] in the "third cultural age" which is that of "God's absence."[3] The proposition of the *Centre Jean-Bart* here runs like this:

"Each man is told to assume the risk of life in the absence of God, because man was meant by the *Other* as capable of taking his own risks."[4]

It is pointless to continue with the quotations: Questions about God are declared meaningless, Nietzsche and Sartre are approved in their revolt against the burden of God, and in the place of a "fixist" religion, "research" and "hope" are recommended. At any rate, behind the somewhat discreet program of the St. Louis colloquium we must read the ultraradical statements of Fr. Talec who, with others, is the manager of the Jean Bart Center.

The crisis that the one illustrates and other registers as acute consists really of three parts:

(a) the content of the "new religion" and the powerful propaganda behind it;

(b) the pressure, influence and quasidomination of the new religion's adepts among the clergy, thus in every nook and cranny of the Church and religious life;[5]

(c) the masses of Christians, lay and ecclesiastic, whose attitude varies within the gamut of confusion, consternation, despair, violent reaction, apostasy, indifference, disaffection.

It is then legitimate, indeed urgent, to ask—not what the "concerned layman" can do, since this book is emphatically not an activist's manual—what is the Christian's position in the Church which is clearly threatened by the danger of becoming another Church in its visible presence, perhaps for centuries. The question should be understood as formulated in somewhat the same manner as Cardinal Newman formulated *his* question about the "idea of a university." Newman did not urge the reader to go out and work for or against the university (structure, curriculum, status, discipline) of his time, he indicated what the university *is* essentially, regardless whether it is so now, was so in the past, will be so in the future. Similarly, we are interested here in indicating what the Christian should think of his position as a Christian in the midst of the spiritual/intellectual earthquake affecting and unbalancing him from all sides.

It is neither for the author nor for the readers to define doctrine, morals, tradition, magisterium, or the destination of the Church itself. However, common sense and rationality dictate the view that the twentieth century or the Second Vatican Council did not, could not, represent such a total transformation either of man or of the Church as it is suggested today by some thinkers, prelates, and priests. A transformation under the pressure of which we would have to rethink and redefine, and eventually to cast out, the traditional doctrine, morals, and magisterium. If it were true that the Church had followed the wrong tracks or, the alternate view, that the Church had followed the right tracks of history but that history itself is now mutating, then the conclusion would have to be even more radical than the progressive thinkers assume. For in that case the future cannot be called "humanistic," this word would spell "fixism" too; the future would indeed be so open that no statement whatever could be made about it. Granted, in that case the traditional magisterium would be of no use; but why should one accept then a new magisterium—for example, Hans Küng's view of infallibility rather than the infallibility of the pope? Hence, all considered, it is advisable to choose *some* guidelines in the on-going process of Christian religious life, and such guidelines, if we indeed admit to a general uncertainity, cannot be other than the Christian tradition and teaching. What the progressive theologians do not seem to realize—and this will one day boomerang against them— is that granting a total freedom of "search" for Jesus Christ, people may just return to their earlier orthodox worship. The search then leads to what the Germans call "Ortsbestimmung" (finding out exactly where one is), an effort to take stock. In this process we may ask a number of questions which permits us to restore, so to speak, *being* to our life instead of the *becoming* we are told is the new truth.

Of the worst effects of the earthquake that mangled Christian souls in the last decade and a half, by far the most damaging has been the *confusion:* One by one, all certitudes have been dismantled, almost according to a strategy. The "essentials" must be kept, but the "inessentials" may be jettisoned, trumpeted progressive thinkers already in the early 1960's, and they quoted St. Augustine's dictum about unity, diversity and charity. Yet the line was increasingly blurred between the essentials and the inessentials, so that when the former began to be thrown out on the trashheap of history, a climate of terror was established; the operation was met with a stunned silence. I quote from titles that appeared over a few years in the then (late sixties, early seventies) prestigious publication, *Herder Correspondence,* in order to illustrate how the operation of blurring the line was conducted:

"Must Celibacy be Compulsory?"; "Are Seminaries Essential?"; "The Church in the Ghetto"; "The New Thinking on the Eucharist"; "The Theology of Revolution"; "How Necessary are our Schools?"; "The Future of the Episcopate"; "The Priest's Uncertain Role"; "The Demand for Married Priests"; "Is Intercommunion Possible?"; "Goodbye to the Confessional?"; "New Thinking on Revelation"; "Are Nuncios Necessary?"; etc.

This kind of subtle propaganda for radical change was certainly a powerful factor of creating confusion, but the targets of the operation, the millions of believers, supplied another factor; when one sector of Christians declared the changes intolerable, there was always another sector adding that they go along, although regretfully, since the change in question does not bite into the real meat of doctrine. Thus, Christians were not only confused, they became also divided. A decisive third phase was reached when the question arose just what *is* a Christian, who claims the authority to define it, do all bishops agree with the pope and with tradition, are the "groups of basic search" not more advanced in the work of giving an identity to Christians than the accustomed sources of authority?

The confusion which soon degenerated into despair may only be cleared up by the above-mentioned "Ortsbestimmung," locating where Christianity is now and what directions it can take under the present circumstances. The rest of this chapter attempts to articulate this concern, in the general light of our discussion of Humanism and its inroads in the Christian body, soul, and institutions. This articulation is pertinent to the issue of Humanism and Christian humanism for more than just the so-far discussed reasons. We argued that insofar as the Christian religion permeates western civilization, the triumph of Humanism within the Church inevitably leads to its triumph in secular society also, without any serious countervailing power. Thus, when Christians are alarmed by the emergence of Humanism in the life of their secular institutions (schools, tribunals, media, government departments, etc.) and would like to have recourse against it in the Church as an alternative response, they realize with a sense of horror that such an alternative exists less and less. Catholic schools, Catholic media, Catholic decision-making apparatuses, Catholics advising government departments are hardly distinguishable from the radical secular schools, etc., and often they are even more extreme in their advocacy of causes. This is, after all, the situation toward which were pointing the just-quoted titles of *Herder Correspondence:* the complete assimilation of the Church to the World. And if the World, following its inherent logic, adopts the Humanist ideology, the Church must not hold back. This is where we are: The representatives of the Church, or rather, many of its official voices, speak the humanist tongue. Our task is then two-fold:

(a) recognize this tongue whenever it is used, on the basis of the analysis of humanism performed in Chapters One and Two, while realizing that this tongue is flexibly applicable to all situations, just like the language of true religion. In other words, it is not necessary, not even possible, to examine each situation where Humanism, its intention and terminology, manifests itself, it is sufficient to have a grasp of Humanism as an ideology, a counter-religion, in order to detect its inspiration in statements, directives, projects, assemblies, etc., whether by ecclesiastic or lay personnel, Church or secular institutions;

(b) meet the Humanist thrust relentlessly, the way the Church met the forefathers of Humanism, that is the heresies, in its two thousand year history. This operation needs solid Christians who often must step in for their vacillating Church when the latter's voice is either uncertain or conciliatory vis-a-vis humanism. But these Christians should realize that for all the talk of an adult mankind and of revolutionary mutations the situation reproduces many earlier models: A heresy is gnawing at the entrails of the faith, and this heresy will have to be uprooted.

I.
Is The Traditional Christian View Still Valid?

It is the core of humanistic ideology that man is its exclusive center; in proportion as man is exalted, God is diminished in his absoluteness. We have seen that man's self-exaltation takes the form of worshipping the "new man" whose locus of salvation is the "future." In general, the humanistic position assumes that man is master of his destiny, and if he is not a master in the present conditions, he must do everything to remove the obstacles and assert himself. This leads to the gradual abolition of all that had been held valid before, so that the "new man" emerges as really the "first man." Whether the Joachites in the thirteenth century, or some German pietist theologians (Bengel, Oetinger) in the eighteenth, such men claim to possess the secret key both to Holy Scripture and to History, and see in their own time the wonderful result of preparation by all previous epochs. Thus, they are eminently qualified to prepare the next generation, the last, the end of history. They do not have to be divine to achieve it, only in some sense superhuman, *comprehensores,* in the medieval terminology, elect. Pico assumed no divine status; he merely claimed to know the formula to unlock man's potential divinization. Bengel thought he was the beneficiary of a personal revelation granting him the means to understand the chronology of salvation history. Oetinger asserted that he and his contemporaries are better equipped than the Apostles to decipher the real meaning of the Gospels. Hegel did not suggest that he was a better philosopher than his predecessors, but believed that he had solved the enigma of the connection between the World Spirit and man immersed in historical existence; with his speculative edifice completed, history had come to an end.

Similarly, with certain Christian humanists today. They do not say in so many words that man is now the absolute in the place of God, but they formulate a number of propositions of which such is the logical outcome: They propose that man has come of age, he is now mature; that mature man cannot accept the myths his grandfather lived with; that his conscience must be respected as autonomous, not depending on any external command, whether by the Church as an institution or by the moral law. It is interesting to note that at the time when vigorous and probing minds discover the many servitudes to which modern technology and mind-manipulation subject modern man, progressive theologians begin to glory about science and its techniques, suggesting that mankind has made a decisive leap into what Abbot Joachim used to call *plenitudo intellectus* and Teilhard de Chardin, "noosphere." But the arguments about mankind's maturity are as false today as they were in the twelfth century. Behind them there lurks at all times the humanist impatience and arrogance, also the ignorance-bred haste to push relunctant humanity into a position where his alleged maturity and freedom can be proved—by science, by technology, and by the refusal of his *status creaturae.*

The affirmation of everybody's personal autonomy within the Church leads to the dismantlement of the whole doctrinal edifice. If (modern) man is master of his conscience in matters of doctrine, faith, and morals, then why and to whom should he confess, why should he see in communion the presence of Christ, why should he follow a Church-taught moral law? Carried away by his own eloquence, Meister Eckhart in the fourteenth century preached that Jesus is resurrected in man's soul; today we may not even be sure that progressive theologians who speak of just such an "individualized" Jesus mean the same God resurrected in each soul.

Things do not always take this excessive form. "Maturity" is often interpreted these days as the fact of receiving communion standing, in the hand rather than on the tongue; of rejecting marriage in favor of looser forms of cohabitation; of assuming that the Mass is a commemorative event; of suggesting in catechisms the equivalence of all religions; etc. These and other examples may indeed seem to be "inessential." Only when we understand the ideological roots of such practices can we uncover the dynamics of apparently disconnected and innocuous changes. The examples could be multiplied to cover the area of priestly celibacy, of birth control, seminary courses, and so on, but the important thing is to emphasize that behind the radical proposals there is no sudden and intellectually honest awareness that some ecclesiastical practices are defective, but humanist-ideological arguments taking the same direction in vastly different historical contexts. Remember that Joachim proclaimed that his contemporaries, at least the monks, are mature for a spiritual mutation, that so did Lessing six hundred years later (disqualifying, by the way, the Joachites' claim), and so did Teilhard de Chardin two hundred years after Lessing. If, with slight variations, the main propositions and supporting arguments are always the same, one does well to conclude that the historical period has nothing to do with the issue and that the will to absolutize man is a permanent project, in fact the essence of idolatry. In other words, Church matters and mundane matters can hardly be *now* so excessively evil as to invite a total rethinking and revolution, since Joachim's *now,* Lessing's or Bengel's *now,* the *now* of Hegel, Marx, or Teilhard, different as they were in their terminological garb, sparked an identical reaction on the part of their followers. Thus, the absurdity of the humanist position has two effects:

(a) it gives away the game which is to seize on any evil (alas, a frequent occurrence) to proclaim an age ripe for a radical transformation; and

(b) it authorizes the critics, by its excessive claims, to present the counterclaim, namely that the traditional Christian view is at least as valid, without being time-bound, as the alternatives so insistently and aggressively urged.

The question of the "validity" of the Christian religion cannot be treated as that of a political program, a school curriculum, an administrative decree. While there is development in the Church, this development can never be measured by reference to the times and to changed conditions. The truth–content of the Christian religion is not comparable to that, for example, of the Pythagorean sect in ancient Southern Italy where debates were settled by reference to what the Master had said: *ipse dixit.* The content of the Christian religion is divinely revealed but, considered also in itself, it is the most accurate set of statements that one may hold about man's nature, about the balance between faith and reason, the interior and the exterior man, the condition on which society rests, human relations. Doctrinal development means not a revamping of the Christian religion, but the unraveling, as new questions arise not yet seen in a new context, of what the doctrine in its human richness contains and explicits. At the same time, (as an earlier-quoted passage from Yves Congar indicates,) there are parts of doctrine and structure that cannot change and must be preserved intact.

Let us examine three examples of change and permanence. The *prevention of human life* (eugenics, abortion, mechanical contraception) is forever contrary to the Christian religion, no matter how circumstances change: demographically, relative to poverty, or otherwise. The removal of the sanctity of life interferes with several commandments, with incarnation, and with the proper understanding of sexuality in the hedonistically inclined human being. The usual argument—why are Christians allowed to kill in war and inflict capital punishment on criminals—is not valid because just as the individual has a right to life, so has the community: it is duty-bound to protect itself and take the life of the attacker if no other means are available.

The second example is meant to illustrate the area of conceivable change which is however prudentially not advisable and therefore improbable. *Celibacy* was not always demanded of members of the clergy. The abuses became however so scandalous and the cases so numerous that it became an enforced requirement. Can one, with this variation in mind, suggest a return to a married priesthood, especially with an ecumenic objective in mind, since the Greco-Orthodox and Protestant churches do not impose celibacy rules? On the face of it, this is an "inessential" area where changes in the surrounding style of life might suggest a modification of existing rules. Yet the question legitimately arises: Should priests not stand apart from, and above the surrounding general mores so as to render the all-important service of a model to the community? That priests used to be married is a weak argument: The meaning of *tradition,* properly understood, is that the Church does not have to be periodically reformed, going back to the origins: It is always in an organic relationship with those origins through an uninterrupted continuity. The fact that the communities visited by Paul, the earliest ones, acknowledged a married priesthood is compatible with the Church's later decision that chastity is the best condition for priests.

The third example is taken from the area of change which, in order to have meaning, must be viewed against permanence as its background. The bishops, for centuries selected among white men, today represent all races. Black,

Hindu, Chinese, Indians are made bishops in large numbers, in recognition of two facts: that their respective races occupy a new and growing historical role, and that is is part of this process that their elites are present in all the endeavors of public life. These people and races did not recently become "mature" through some change of substance, but they have entered upon a state of institutional existence (statehood, nationhood) which they lacked for a long time. The Church, also an institution, must recognize this historic change and deal with these nations through their own representatives. This is neither racism nor hypocrisy; the measure is similar to the one taken by a government which at one point recognizes the corporate existence of groups. The Church itself is incapable of promoting such a corporate existence; it can only recognize it when it becomes a fact.

The three examples here listed would normally find the humanist in opposition. There is no difference among the cases, he would say, the distinctions are artificial. If man is free—and Christianity did hardly anything in order to emancipate him—then he has all the rights, none of them may be taken away from him. In other words, mothers possess the right to abort, priests the right to marry, and all nations the right to have bishops chosen among them. The delineation of nuances only shows that the Church is still not free and humane; it shies away from sexual problems— it is "sexist" in words and deeds—but opportunistically quick when it comes to make friends with classes and races it previously ignored.

What the humanist does not appreciate in his absolutization of man is precisely the Church's wise understanding of man as a frail and multifaceted creature, with a strong inclination to sin, yet one who, when aided with external props, is capable of choosing the right course. For the humanist, man is either an absolute being *now* or a potential absolute in the *future*. For Christianity, man is forever imperfect—not unfinished, waiting for maturation—but is not a Godforsaken wretch. With reference to the three cases briefly discussed, the humanist cannot go along with the conception that in questions about life powerless creatures— the child in its mother's uterus, the sick and the aged, and all people in their ordinary state, must be protected, while, for the same reason, the offenders against the community's safety—external enemies or criminals—may be deprived rightfully of their life, since the community too is rightly protected by its soldiers and policemen. Similarly, it is a scandal for the humanist that the Church is immersed in history, thus follows in its institutional policy some of the patterns that the course of human events concretely recommends: the naming of Black bishops, for example, when in the political order Blacks constitute States, become educated, enter the professions; or the Christianization of pagan shrines, as it happened in many parts of Europe and of South America; the acceptance of many local practices to which a population—Indians on the high plateaus of Peru or Guatemala, the people of Naples, etc., is traditionally accustomed and wherein no moral harm is done, and so on. On the other hand, the Church cannot accept or "Christianize" practices which contradict its teaching: It can never countenance polygamy, the exposition or killing of children, the massacre of the old, the trial-marriage, and other not infrequent customs past or present. In the humanist's reductionist perspective these distinctions are artificial and must be bound to sordid interests in which the Church shares with the ruling classes, superstitious old women, or the distributors of social privileges. It is thus not even a question that of the two: the Christian religion and humanism, only the first has a rich, varied and nuanced view of man; the second sees a monolith, free or unfree, master or slave, God or nothing. The question is implicitly answered: Which one has a greater respect for man, the ideology which absolutizes him or the teaching attentive to his abundant gifts, penchant for evil, and multifaceted soul.

II.
Catechism, Magisterium, Infallibility

These three words used to be rocks in a raging sea, as the saying goes; today they seem precarious, exposed to mockery, indifference, abolition. The fever of reinterpretation has not spared them; indeed it might be said that if the "inessentials" were the first targets of humanist critics, they were mere stepping stones to a more comfortable platform from which to bombard the impregnable truths, the "essentials." The question is, once again, is the critique valid? Must the sacraments be rethought, researched? Has the Christian religion come to a point where, because of the traditional teaching and practices, it can no longer attract the avant-garde of thinking man?

In an article over a decade ago, Karl Rahner suggested that the Church was no longer able to draw to itself the urban intellectuals, and is thus condemned to remain the half-superstition, half-religion of old peasant women lighting piously a candle in the dark corner of a village church. Such a statement is both malevolent and false. Malevolent (and un-Christian) because God does not discriminate among souls, the peasant woman's fervor is as precious to him as that of the professor or the journalist. In the second place, what Rahner said is untrue because even since he had written these words, there have been spectacular cases of conversion by radical and skeptic intellectuals. I mention only Malcolm Muggeridge, the English writer, formerly unbelieving editor of *Punch,* and Maurice Clavel, brilliant French writer and professor, whose conversion in the middle of a turbulent life has turned him into a defender of the faith and acerbic critic of indifferentist, permissive bishops and clergy. And, of course, there is Alexander Solzhenitsyn, not properly a convert of recent vintage, but a spiritual and moral giant in whose sweep legions of young intellectuals (notably the "new philosophers" in France) have been turning away from their Marxist or free-thinking aberrations. These are the well-known and well-publicized cases; but there are many more such intellectuals (let us mention them only, since this is what Rahner hankers after), at least two dozen known to me in the circle of acquaintances, although so young that they are not yet publicly famous. These illustrations are, however, not likely to change Rahner's mind, since if an intellectual becomes a convert to the defective and un-progressive Church, he becomes automatically identified by Rahner with the silently praying old peasant woman! The bad faith of humanist clergy is brought to broad daylight as they distinguish among the faithful those attached to the "old" Church and those who wish to go on "experi-menting" in view of the future. The first group, because it is "fixist," is *ipso facto* despised; the second group, because it is "in search of what it is to be a Christian," is surrounded with solicitude.

Thus, the three words in the title, and some others that the reader is invited to supply, may be seen in the proper light. It is not true, for example, that there is a crisis in the recruitment of priests: If the seminaries were serious places of sacerdotal preparation, disciplined instead of lax, a large number of young men, having faith and vocation, thirsting for truth and the ordered life, would be happy to get in. If the bishops made it clear that *vocation* is not *commitment* (the latter being the Sartrian *engagement,* by definition revocable as new meanings of life are discovered), the desire for permanent loyalty lodged in the soul would overcome in priests the sexual urge and would dissuade them from leaving their functions and getting married. If the Mass were not allowed to degenerate into mere fashionable per-formances, churches today would be full, as they are when the traditional Mass is celebrated, even at the small hours of the morning or at places difficult of access.

If, in spite of these evidences, the humanist clergy takes the other course: lax seminaries, absurd or indecent experi-mental mass, games played with the doctrine, etc.—it is be-cause they have been persuaded by their mentors that

(a) the Church must be dissolved in the now perfected world;

(b) be a Christian is to believe in man; and

(c) to be a man is to adopt the life-style of modern hedonists.

It is obvious that in spite of a superficial similarity of language, habits, and gestures, the humanist theologian, prelate, priest and lay Christian do not have the same Church, sacraments, and magisterium in mind as the orthodox Christian. The latter calls upon the former—whose motivations and attitudes he does not usually understand as inspired by a new religion—in the name of a faith and of concepts which for the humanist are often a faint memory, an embarrassing reminder, in one word, a nuisance. This is not to say that the "humanist" Christian belongs already to another faith, philosophy and magisterium, at least not in the majority of cases. Probability is that the "humanist" priest or layman is a hesitant figure, impressed by the "modern world," although reluctant to change his personal "commitment" unless it is made easy for him. Such people may be, for all we know, the majority in all institutions, enterprises, bureaucracies and churches. They yield not to reflective conviction but to fashion, snobbism, pressure, the magnets of conformism; they can function in the spirit of orthodoxy only if steadied by firmness and authority. Otherwise, they drift on the ocean of permissiveness and find a certain inner satisfaction in the mistaken belief that by being disobedient, they are free. But, as Kierkegaard has written, the clergy's disobedience is not a sign of intellectual search for an independent viewpoint, it is merely unruliness, the consequence of an uncertain authority exercised over it. St. Bernard can be quoted here again who, a great knower of souls, had written to a bishop that not to use his authority is worse than making mistakes in its exercise.

The crisis—in Greek the word means "separation"—in the Church is then to be sought in the *two languages* used, that of orthodoxy and that of humanism; it is immeasurably aggravated by the fact that the existing authority makes no serious efforts to heal the rupture by reimposing *one language*. This brings us back to the three words in the title of this section.

Why is infallibility questioned? It is said that modern man, that is the one shaped by humanism, living in a democratic, pluralistic society, accustomed to discuss every issue from politics to science, cannot accept what St. Augustine formulated as *Roma locuta causa finita,* Rome has spoken, the case is closed. Fact is, however, modern man has lived in democratic, pluralistic societies only for about a century, in reality between 1860 and 1930, in a few small parts of the world. It is certainly not a habit that mankind has adjusted to, since even before the "hundred years" were up, many countries reverted to other types of regimes, ranging from mildly authoritarian to monolithic. This turn away from democratic pluralism may or may not have taken place with the citizens' consent, but it did take place; it is as genuine or nongenuine as the choice of democracy was a hundred years ago.

In the second place, even in times when the magisterium was firmly exercised in matters of faith and morals, the scientific, scholarly and political discourse was remarkably free. There can be no more free discussion of topics in philosophy, theology, astronomy, politics, etc., than in the works of such thinkers as William of Ockham and Nicholas of Cusa; their freedom of intellectual innovation was in no sense curtailed by the *de facto* recognized (*de iure* only since Vatican I, in 1870) papal infallibility. The latter was so clearly recognized, in spite of the opposition from several corners, that Ockham's younger contemporary, Marsilius of Padua, wrote his important work, *Defensor Pacis,* to suggest conciliar infallibility instead. Cusanus himself was a "conciliarist" in his youth, but abandoned his views later and became a supporter of papal infallibility, the guarantee, as he saw it, of a true ecumenism.

In short, for this issue no arguments may be derived from

contemporary events or from mental habits assimilated in other areas of discourse. Examples abound for great scientists who disagree on issues in their field, then accept humbly the infallible papal pronouncements about doctrinal and moral matters. The order of knowledge is not the same in, let us say, ethics and physics. We may speak of an implicit infallibility that the Church always asserted it possessed as a charisma, but explicitly stated only in 1870, following the law of development of doctrine, discussed before, which states that there are no *new* doctrinal truths, only opportune explicitations of what has been implicit.

Without assuming the fact of papal infallibility, it would be hard to justify the magisterium and catechism. The Christian religion, like every religion, has a teaching function. In the humanist perspective such a function would be impossible to perform. Teaching presupposes a set of facts organized in a coherent fashion and assumed to remain what they are—or, with the principle of the orderly transformation of these facts given, assumed to change in an orderly manner. All sciences adopt one of these two methods. However, the modern humanist's future-orientedness is so radical that, after denying fixity and being, it is unable to produce a principle of change and becoming. The quasi-magisterium that humanism now claims to assume for itself cannot crystallize because it postulates change for its own sake, in other words it assumes that it is not *something* that changes, but change itself. The method, if it is one, may be compared to the ideal of progressive educators who want to teach "mobility." But mobility can be taught only in reference to something stable which serves as a measure of the principle of change. When such a principle is not supplied, change becomes a circular motion, in other words merely a different kind of immobility.

The true objective of the usurped magisterium, hence of catechisms, too, which translate its directives to children's use, is not the enthronement of ceaseless change, it is the setting up of a new Church. The emphasis on "future" and "hope" becomes a bait, a bridge helping the enthusiast to opt against fixity which is the general label applied to the "old" Church. It is like the political systems promising the permanent revolution: If revolution means unexpected novelty, then these systems certainly make no room for it since even the counter-revolution, also a novelty, would have to be authorized or at least envisaged as legitimate. In fact, however, the "permanent revolution" means the continuation of the initial impetus and motive, it demands that all future revolutions be launched on the already set tracks. The progressive catechisms now proposed, together with their prototype, the Dutch Catechism, are increasingly bold statements of a new religion, not re-statements of orthodox truths supposedly rephrased for easier comprehension by modern man. "Modern man" himself, as we have suggested, is not, in the humanist's eye, the permanent man living in a new civilization, he is the post-Christian man, who has performed a kind of existentialist leap outside the God-created human being. Why be surprised then that the authors of new catechisms, new prayers, new experiments, or the episcopal participants at Pentecostal celebrations promote a parallel religion, modelled after Christianity, but only in a manner that a caricature imitates the original.

III.
Is There Still a Place for Christians?

In a way, this question has been answered in the two preceding sections: a catholic cannot be a Catholic *alone,* he sees himself as member of a corporation, the mystical body. Moreover, he must be a member of the Church, in communion with pope, bishops, and clergy. Thus, insofar as we have argued that the Christian view is still valid, without in any sense weakened by the wear and tear of history, the attacks of humanists, the frenzy of radical mutationists, insofar as we have argued that there is no

ground for the abolition of magisterium and infallibility—
we have implicitly stated that there is as big a place for
orthodox Christians in the twentieth century as there was
in the first, the tenth, or the sixteenth. This is true of the
Christian religion as well as of the values of Christian civilization. If, as it is evident, the present century and civilization make gigantic efforts to eliminate even the traces of
Christian civilization in favor of totalitarian barbarism and
liberal hedonism, this is just one more added and potent
reason for upholding the pertinent values and trying to
reinsert them in the two deviant forms.

In the *Letter to Diognetes* (cca 120 A.D.), the anonymous
author[6] who seems to instruct a candidate for conversion,
explains to him that Christians are good citizens precisely
because they are *in* this world but not *of* this world. At
the time, one great point of attack against Christians was
that by refusing to sacrifice to the Roman gods and to
participate in the official emperor-worship, they made themselves enemies of the country likely to bring disaster upon
the empire. The *Letter* demonstrates that loyalty to the true
God and the observance of the moral law attached to his
name, are better guarantees of honest service to society
than any mechanical gesture that the pagans distractedly
perform.

It would be desirable to address a letter to a twentieth-
century Diognetes about the justification of Christian life
in today's neopagan societies. This time it would have to
be a matter not merely of informing a future convert that
he may remain a loyal Roman after he ceases being a
pagan; the urgent task today is to reassure Christians that
even though society reverts to paganism, they owe it to
Church and society to remain good Christians. It is, of
course, an old story that at numerous times it was the
laity that lifted the common cause of Christianity out of
the crisis. Vatican II indeed placed a great emphasis on
the layman's role, more, his initiative, in Church matters. It shows the strength and self-confidence of the hu-

manists that they succeeded in turning this pastoral policy to their own advantage, by

(a) isolating the traditional believers from Church-integrated lay action; and

(b) encouraging the radical innovators among the laity to take the leadership of "basic groups," as if to demonstrate that Catholics are unanimous in demanding a radical mutation.

Orthodox Catholics have remained, in consequence, doubly abandoned: by a substantial segment of the clergy which went over to the humanist side, and by the Church's traditional hierarchy which is often too timid to offer protection. We are today perhaps at a crossroads in modern Church history. It will be some time before loyal Christian believers take an exact inventory of their situation and organize themselves. What should they presuppose before reasserting an authentic Christian life, inside the Church and in the civilization of which the Church must remain a guiding part, since not only souls but the realities affecting them too must be Christianized. The answer that ours are pluralistic societies is hardly a serious objection: It has not prevented the humanists from attempting, too often successfully, to bend the plural structures in their own favor, in fact, to declare that mankind's civilization must become universally humanist. In the second place, Roman society of the imperial age was also pluralistic: Pagan, Greek, and a multitude of oriental trends and creeds intermingled; there were among them clash and cooperation. This did not mean that the Christians retired from the hope of influencing the outcome, even at the cost of persecution. When present-day humanists and their Christian allies call upon Christians or the Church to "respect" the existing pluralism, they act like the Roman imperial administration when it issued the ultimatum: Either worship Caesar or die in the circus.

We may see three points worth considering when we examine the matter of reaffirming Christianity in Church and society:

(1) The last flickers of liberal/tolerant society still prevent the persecution of loyal Christians. One should not be hypnotized by the Roman-imperial sound of the term "persecution"—but at the same time one might also wonder about the strange recurrence: Christians *are* persecuted under communist regimes as they used to be in the Roman days. It is even worse because there were then periods of persecution between those of Nero, the first, and Diocletian, the last. During the intervals, Christianity prospered and spread. In today's Marxist regimes, the persecution is active and never-relenting State policy: The Christian who does not sacrifice to the communist Caesar—by cooperating with the official ideology, by not having his children baptized, by not going to church, by refraining from religious practice— loses his job or misses his promotion, may not find a place to live, sees his wages blocked, his children deprived of a higher education, etc.

True, Christians are not persecuted by the liberal-tolerant society. Yet, we have documented here a subtle form of persecution, at times amounting to spiritual and moral terror, which does not emanate directly from the institutions but from desacralized society's influence on the media, the schools, the legislators, and members of the clergy. On the one hand, offensive and blasphemous films and plays, immorality taught in schools, and antihuman laws, on the other hand the liquidation of doctrine and morals, the dismantlement of structures, the undermining of things sacred. These parallel phenomena are united in purpose since the common inspiration is humanistic. The novelty is not the presence of this inspiration in the fabric of society, it is the rapidity with which entire segments of the Church and of Christian values succumb to it. The Christian who meets it for the first time, let us say as a parent, hears his complaints dismissed and is told it is time for him to leave his "ghetto"; he hardly notices that he is thereby compelled to enter a bigger "ghetto," secular society now encompassing the Church too and blind to Christian truth.

Thus, it is easy to comprehend the renewed relevance of the *Letter to Diognetes,* of the message contained therein. It is that Christians, living in time but also in view of eternity, must not succumb to the temptation of thinking that with the present triumphs of humanism the "game is up," that the victories of the false prophets are either final or capable of changing the framework of history. To be a good man, a good citizen, a good Christian never loses an ounce of its timeliness; and one must hasten to add that "good" here is understood in the evangelical sense.

The injunction to remain in this world with hope and good works remains a valid one, for two reasons:

(a) the first is that Christianity is not a this-worldly system of salvation-through-utopia which prescribes the sacrifice of generations for a final abstract happiness. Every soul is as valuable as every other soul, every life must be given the chance of being made into a good life. Thus, the Christian doctrine intrinsically teaches the importance of the here and now, the opportunities given to each to make his salvation, thus the charity toward other men through channels that society makes available;

(b) the second reason is historical: What impressed the Romans, neighbors, leaders of society, finally Caesar, was the Christians' unbroken solidarity and continued good reputation in spite of the calumnies spread about them by certain hostile circles. Reading the works of scholars like Harnack, Samuel Dill, Labriolle, retracing minutely the history of relationships between pagan Rome and the Christian sect, one is struck by the unceasing attacks that Roman and Greek authors launched against the Christians, their morals, their superstitions, their absurd practices. The calumniatory line is uninterrupted up to and including the Emperor Julian, not because each author researched the case anew, but because one borrowed from the other the standard arguments and case-histories. Christians engage in incest, eat unclean food, are cowardly, secretive; even what they do openly is grotesque: They worship a dead criminal, are stupid, etc. Slowly, however, another line becomes obvious too, and if the emperors finally decided that the emancipation of Christianity, and soon its rise to the status of state religion, is a good thing, this must have been because more trustworthy reports had reached their ears than the stereotyped ones colported by the writers and intellectuals.[7]

In short, the Christian, unlike the Hegelian, the Marxist, the Humanist, is aware that history is not a one-directional process, with evil, or matter, or selfishness, or idolatry left behind in proportion as mankind enters into goodness, purity, knowledge and wisdom, but rather an album with pictures, showing more or less similar people in many varieties, no picture decisively better than others, and many with recurring themes. Just as the "persecution of Christians" is not a thing past without the possibility of being renewed, so the emergence from persecution, and steadfastness while it lasts, are not to be excluded. More, steadfastness and the end of persecution must be envisaged and actively promoted.

(2) It would be unwise to ignore here any of the temptations to which ordinary Christians, as individuals and groups, are exposed on account of the infiltration in the Church of humanist ideology. One such temptation was just now discussed: the doubt that Christianity continues to be valid, or, put differently, the doubt that the radical humanists may not have history with its manifest apparatus working for them today. The other temptation—and their common source is always the greatest temptation of all, despair—is to regard oneself as part of a rearguard, the "remnant," who by tenacity and luck survive the shipwreck, but only to be now tossed about in a fragile lifeboat, with no shore in sight. The remnant-mentality is an alternative to the other desperate road, schism, and it is, naturally, the better branch of the alternative. Yet, it too follows from a logic which leads away from the affirmation implicit in the letter to Diognetes.

This logic is that of men and women who persuaded themselves—justifiably according to appearances—that the end of the road has come and that their faith, while alone valid, is slowly reduced to the status of folklore or museum piece. They do not notice that this belief is the mirror image of the humanist thesis: The traditional Church, writes Hans Küng, served the European populations acceptably until the later Middle Ages, but became then an increasingly embarrassing and tyrannical burden on their shoulder. Today, he advises, the Church must be modern, integrate married priests and women priests, trust youth in matters of sexual options, and back socialist "experiments" like the recent ones in Cuba and Chile. Like the masochist to his tormentor, the remnant is irresistibly attracted to the picture so presented, he accepts in advance to figure on it in the role assigned to him. What he ought to say to himself instead is that the obvious silliness of Küng's thesis—in a book hailed as a kind of modern Summa[8] —disqualifies his and his confreres' discourse from being taken seriously by Christians and by rational men generally. Indeed, in many of its passages, Küng's book and dozens like it, read like pages borrowed from the Humanist Manifestoes, past and present. This fact ought to reassure Christians with a penchant to join the "remnant," because they ought to know that their religion's survival is guaranteed not only by Christ, also by its extraordinary understanding of the human soul. There may be Christian sects based on unreason, irrationality, and a wrong appraisal of human nature, but with the Catholic religion reason will always occupy a royal role. Küng and those who misuse the Catholic knowledge and insights cannot be right; their commotion will fade into oblivion, following that of the Brethren of the Free Spirit and a Pico's sophistications.

Yet, "remnantism" continues, in the shadow of the Küngs, inseparable from them. Upon analysis, its adepts display two features:

(a) They adopt the supplicant tone of those aware of defeat, and refer to themselves as beaten dogs, victims, exiles from paradise. They complain that bishops mistreat them, *and* seize every opportunity to beg these bishops to bestow on them their favors. To be concrete, on one page of magazine *X* we find the detailed denunciation of the new mass (for example), on the next page the humble request that the celebration of the old mass be permitted:

(b) impressed by their imposed and assumed function as victims, the members of the remnant no longer grasp the essence of their freedom as Christian men. Again concretely, they do not seem to know—or do not trust their knowledge—that (for example) Christians need no special approval for holding and attending the traditional mass. To be sure, they ought not to cause scandal; but when a scandalous situation is officially tolerated, the supposed scandalmonger is, in fact, the rectifier. If the remnant studied Church history, it would realize the freedom with which Christian scholars, priests and laymen alike discussed the issue of papal heresy (that of fourteenth-century popes John XXII, Benedict and Clement), the theses of Duns Scotus and Oresme, of St. Thomas himself. Etienne Gilson writes of his amazement that Nicholas of Cusa was never called before the Inquisition.

The danger of being reduced to a "remnant" is to end up a schismatic. The psychological preconditions are present since people with a remnant-mentality see themselves as a small and shrinking group, with truth held in their hands until it must be defended against all others. But truth not in the open and openly confessed and lived by becomes a secret knowledge, something like a gnosis whose adepts invent signs for internal recognition by the initiates. This is precisely the strategy of the humanists: to make Christians feel and live their minority status in the Church, to make them accept with resignation the place of Rahner's old peasant woman over against the humanist who can then safely occupy the place of the urban intellectual. We said that the old peasant woman's soul is as valuable as that of the city sophisticate; anyway, it is not the humanist's function to assign places, to reserve some for his self-defined "modern man" while relegating others to dark corners of the Church.

(3) It follows from the Christian's duty of self-affirmation in the Church and in the world that he must not shy away from politicising his position to a certain degree. What ultimately impressed the Roman emperors was not the Christians' charity and good reputation; it was the power they represented. The author of the letter to Diognetes knew nothing about it; he wrote almost two centuries before the great occurrence. We are told, and we naturally agree, that Christianity is not a political creed and that a Christian political–party is, if not an intrinsic contradiction, at least a perilous and precarious bridge between two entities which do not mix. This does not mean, however, that, without forming any sort of party in the parliamentary or other sense of the term, Christians should not let their weight be felt as a cohesive and militant group. Again: within the Church and within society. What gave the Christian centuries, the thirteenth and the seventeenth, their triumphant character and extraordinary spiritual achievements, was that the men of faith were not timid to assert their right to salvation *and* to conditions facilitating it."The meek shall inherit the earth"—yes, but there is a point where militancy does not contradict meekness. Francis, Ignatius, John of the Cross, the Curé d'Ars were meek, or rather humble men, but it would be a gross mistake to picture them making concessions to those who lock the door of the Church in their face.

There are a number of organizations of Christians on every continent which retain the Christian virtues of humility, patience, obedience, *and* do not let their place be usurped. They are not groups of angels, as if only white purity were allowed to confront pitch blackness. But their membership in France, in Brazil, in Germany, in England, in Africa, in the United States, in Australia—consists of the kind of Christians about whom the letter to Diognetes was written. They fulfill a vital function, qualified perhaps as a mission: to give the fainthearted courage and warn the arrogant. This mission cannot be accomplished from the remnant's back rows, only from the nearest place to the altar.

IV.
Are the Evils of Today New?

The Abbot Joachim regarded the Gospels as so imperfect that he predicted the imminence of a Third Age. Men had obviously not been cured of their sins by Christianity, so the ways of Jesus Christ had to be corrected—and this was the task of St. Francis, according to his radical disciples, the "fraticelli." The number of Christians who found their times filled with intolerable evil in need of an instant and drastic cure is as large as membership in unorthodox movements, sects, and heresies. But are the evils of any given period greater than those of other periods, and is one justified to proclaim the present evil so incomparably immense that it reveals either God's indifference or the imperfection of his design? In either case, man is justified in setting up a new religion under an improved god.

Nobody denies the specific evils of our time: death camps, nuclear annihilation, desperate refugees from fanatic ideologies—yet it seems that the ways mankind has always tried in an effort to mitigate evils are not in need of a drastically new method. This does not mean that the available methods are ever sufficient, that they do more than skim the surface, apply local cures and temporary relief. It only means that there is always between the evils of the time and the remedial action what seems to be a constant ratio; this is quite understandable since it is the same humanity which engenders the evil and which tries to apply the healing

forces. This ratio is extremely modest: very little of the
existing evil is relieved; moreover, when it is at point *A,* its
recrudescence in some other form can be observed at point
B. There is some, to man unknown, universal chemistry at
work: when one corner of the planet finds conditions satis-
factory and has eliminated famine, torture, slavery, persecution, they reappear at the antipodes or in the neighborhood.
And since few people are capable of thinking in global
terms—in spite of the refinements of telecommuncation—the
local satisfaction usually goes together with ignorance of
silent or silenced sufferers elsewhere.

This is true of the Church also. The humanistically
inclined churchmen, like their lay confrères, adopt the language of radicals when they insist on instant and thorough
remedies to the "third world's" backwardness and abuses,
and go so far as to concoct a "theology of revolution"
from bits and pieces of tendentious literature and outright propaganda. The last thing they are interested in ap-
plying are Christian standards of charity. Yet, in my travels
in underdeveloped countries I found the long-resident missionaries to be the most effective healers of evil, true special-
ists of the soul, of the needs of body and society. Nevertheless, their accomplishments are now under attack, and the
missionaries are accused of suppressing the local personality
of the populations as well as of secretly guarding western
imperialist interests. Thus, the bias formed in western radical
circles concerning the "evils of today's world" is built into
the Christian humanist perspective also.

Two conclusions may be derived from these observations.
One is that there is no need to devise new approaches—
radical, thorough, definitive, consecrated by a new theology
—for curing of evil in the world, since this evil is a constant, and the modicum of remedy is at all times available.
It is ordinary human blindness, bias, and other limitations
which block its effective, although also only limited, applica-
tion. Who knows but that the discovery of a universal

panacea—claimed today both by Marxist ideologues and western technocrats—might not extend and deepen the existing evil, even engender new ones. This is not to say that we ought to remain passive in the face of evil, only that we should be humble enough not to think in terms of panaceas, ideological, technological, or humanistic. What is done in leprosariums, orphanages, trade schools and maternity centers run by the Church all over the world penetrates immeasureably deeper and has more durable good effects than Che Guevara's instant guerrilla among the Bolivian peasants or the vast sterilization program enforced recently by the government of India.[9]

The second conclusion is that, as Christ said, the poor will always remain in our midst. We might add that always different people will be "the poor," and not categories or classes like the proletariat or low-salaried women. The *poor* that Christ meant are the all-time victims of the *rich,* but the first are not necessarily the indigent nor the second the men of means. The rich are those who dominate situations, define the terms for others, take over the leading roles, shout the loudest, order others around, claim to speak in their name. The poor are the modest and the weak, the confused and the timid, the ones calling for help but whose lip movements we see as through a glass darkly, or not at all, so we pass. The rich are the media which determine the news, the hard-eyed priests who mock the "sociological Catholics" and their piety, the French Abbé Marc Oraison for whose psychoanalytic teaching Christ represents the genital form of religion. The poor are always the "others" whom the world treats like abstractions, figures on a chart, stomachs to be filled, women to be aborted, case histories to be studied, problems to be solved. Essentially, the role of the poor is to supply the rich with a good conscience. And the rich are always the same, whether called pharisee, catechist-*cum*-sex, bureaucrat, or fashionable theologian.

V.
Ought the Church To Correct Its Course?

If one reads books like Hans Küng's, listens to Karl
Rahner's sermons, observes Fr. Talec's methods of running the Centre Jean-Bart, learns from the Dutch Cathechism
or attends meetings like that of Detroit in 1976, the conclusion is inevitable that in the Church stone is not to remain on stone. Hardly a word in all this verbiage and gesti-
culation about the needs of God, only about those of man:
his needs as a young person, as a sexual being, as a worker, as a Black man, as a woman, as a protesting priest, as
a homosexual, as an atheist. It is not hard to conclude
that if so much is wrong with the Church and in fact with
the Christian religion, then the most modest concession
Church and Christianity may make is entirely to change
course. Crowds of new guides volunteer to show the way.

Must one really hunt down the supposed evils in all the
avenues opened up by these eager guides? Or can one suggest a more simple explanation, namely, that most of the
radical critics, in Church and out, have lost their faith?
A delicate problem is thereby raised. Could we say that the
Abbot Joachim had lost his faith in Christ when he implicitly deprecated the New Testament as representative of
one age, like the Old Testament had been of a previous
age, and insisted on its supersession by the "eternal gospel"? Joachim was a medieval man, even his unorthodoxy
was couched in the terms of the Christian faith, he moved
in a Christian ambiance which influenced his thought,
words, acts, and expectations. Could a Joachim today
still retain, if not the orthodoxy of his faith, at least its
cultural expression—or would he mechanically slip into the
secular, the Marxist, the relativist or the structuralist language of his culture? We see that after a pathetic, long or
short struggle with their background and conscience, the
modern Joachims divest themselves of the Christian language which is no longer supported by a Christian culture,

and begin speaking one or the other fashionable dialect of the "humanistic" language. Why not suppose, since we are told that man lives the way he believes, that these men have also lost their faith—as indeed they usually admit it to a trusted friend or in an unguarded moment. I am told that Hans Küng has made such an admission, and added that if he were ever to recover his faith he would become a "traditionalist." An extraordinarily revealing statement, the interpretation of which is easy: There are only two positions in religious matters: atheism or orthodox belief. If not Sic, then Non; if not Non, then Sic. There are no half-way houses for the Christian Hamlets.

What other indications are there that these men are no mere critics *inside,* but having lost their Christian faith, they are demolishers from *outside*? The fact that they have retained the need for faith, although now a faith other than the Christian. There is an interesting phenomenon here, worth considering. Faith is—also—submission, and these men are unable to submit to something they no longer trust, that their like-minded friends despise, and that the civilization around them neutralizes or outright nullifies. The contemporary texts from which I have quoted earlier (Moltmann, Rahner, Küng, Hulsbosch, etc.) differ radically from the older texts (Joachim, Ockham, Nicholas of Cusa, etc.) in that the latter criticise *but* respect, even love the Church, whereas the former criticise *and* display their contempt, even their hatred. Perhaps the authors of the old texts lacked faith too in its integrality, but the Church was still on their horizon; the contemporary authors despise the Church as they despise the "old peasant woman" who does not bring them the glory they derive from associating with prestigious humanist friends and masters. Hence, they join another faith, submit to another magisterium, proclaim another infallibility. Inside and outside the Vatican lists circulate with the names of prelates who have recently joined the Freemasons, other lists with clergy carrying communist party membership cards, yet others, more openly, of priests in the "charistmatic" movement. The case of Cardinal Suenens (of Malines, in Belgium) is well known, who was so impressed with the fervor of Pentecostalists that he arranged for—a mass?—a celebration?—a concelebration?—a happening?—for them in Rome.

How should we read these signs—because read we must instead of blandly assuming that they are hobbies or mere sacrifices to the Zeitgeist? True, in some instances they are only sects of superficiality and fashion, and this kind of thing is not new. Cardinal Bembo at the court of Leo X was known for his infatuation with pagan forms and mythological figures, where he and other prelates assumed ancient names, played ancient games, adopted the ancient style of swearing "by the gods," referred familiarly to Venus and Apollo. There are "Cardinal Bembos" today also, only they do not dress in imitation-toga but in business suit, do not hold imitation-symposia but attend and applaud communist party meetings. But it is not the Bembo-syndrome which is disturbing; it is the obvious loss of faith observed in their actions. The cases of desertion from the Church or from the sacerdotal status are too numerous even for statistics to keep up with. It is intriguing to note the two parallel but contrary movements: As the Catholics find their rites and catechism increasingly diluted, many of them, even from the intellectual elites, convert to Greco-orthodoxy, aspiring for a deeper faith, a stronger discipline, and more reverential channels of approach to God.[10] In contrast, as prelates and priests lose *their* faith, we witness *their* conversion to occult systems like Freemasonry, or to ideologies, that is, to secularized forms of heresy. "Baptism of the Holy Spirit" replaces Catholic baptism, or rather supersedes it as more fundamental, truer. Note that these esoteric systems claim they possess the key to instant "maturity," in fact saintliness, so that the Catholics converting to them are not, literally, devoid of faith,—let us leave aside the opportunistic pseudoconversions which must also be quite numerous—they display impatience with the burden that a believing Christian must carry. And, of course, instant saintliness may also be only a stepping stone to a later secularization by stages.

The point is that the very ones who urge on the Church a complete course correction are shoddy judges of the Church which they had actually left, transferring elsewhere their still existing faith potential. Two things follow:

a) their criticism of the Church is vitiated by their lapsed membership; and

b) their criticism is not made from a pure heart, but from an alien point of view, sect, or movement.[11]

The implication is not that the Church needs no reforming, indeed adapting, but that this should not happen in the direction and from motives prompted by the critics. This would not be reform but the temptation of another creed. There is a true and a false reform of the Church, wrote Fr. Yves Congar, and he calls the false one inconceivable.[12] Let us be clear about the matter: There have always been priests fighting for legitimate secular goals: the independence of their country, for example; others who kept concubines; others who, as prelates, behaved like cruel lords, who burned down monasteries when an abbot displeased them. The variety of evil actions which illustrate the pages of secular history has its parallel on the pages of Church history. These are dreadful acts, contradicting over and over the moral commandments and the ordinary rules of decency. But the line of toleration is reached when such actions are urged to be elevated to the rank of Church policy, church theology.

Let us take the example of the Colombian priest, Camillo Torres, who joined the guerrillas and died gun in hand for land reform. His action constitutes an individual case, to be dealt with according to canon law, charity, the bishop's harshness or indulgence. Long penitence, silence, or mercy ought to be its sequel and conclusion. But for theologians to invent a "theology of revolution" from the sporadic cases on this pattern, there is neither reason nor excuse.

Such a theology is clearly anathema because it displays a perverted *sensum ecclesiae,* an elementary misunderstanding of what religion is about.

What should the Church "reform" or "correct" in a case such as Torres's? Should it set out to pressure the State to pass a land-reform law? If the State resists, should the Church excommunicate the members of the government? And tomorrow when land reform signals its inherent contradictions and abuses, as in Mexico or Tanzania, should the Church again press for a reversal and excommunicate a new set of recalcitrant ministers? Should the Church have its own minister of agriculture in advisory capacity to cabinet members? But what can happen in the area of agriculture can equally well happen in industry, the airlines, foreign relations, transnational companies, labor unions, or telecommunications: Should the Church name its own experts and advise, scold, praise and penalize at every step? Would it still be the Church—or a parallel bureaucracy, duplicating the business of secular authority? The world would be back in the Middle Ages, replaying the long conflict between papacy and empire, between the respective domains of spiritual and temporal powers. Those who clamor for Church involvement each time injustice is committed, would be the first to accuse the Church of attempting to regain its medieval power position.

In consequence, religion, theology, etc., while not ivory-tower issues since the spiritual touches the temporal at too many points for that, must be allowed to keep their independence from areas which would thus acquire the right similarly to penetrate into the doctrinal and moral heart of the Church. The two—spiritual and temporal—naturally intermingle in man and his civilization. But it is better for man not to fall victim to an intellectual confusion, but rather to belong to two orders; it is better for him not to have his problems of agrarian reform (for example) settled by theological injunctions. If agrarian reform, wage disputes, or colonial issues are theologically decided, they may become uncomfortably permanent, rigid, unreformable, thus unchangeable until the next revolution in theology.[13]

We are not engaged on these pages in the eleboration of a program of reforms for the Church. What has been said so far is meant as a warning signal of the points and crossroads where the Church ought not to be urged to correct its course—other than what takes place inside any living institution. The nomination of nonwhite bishops and the general integration of all races into the institutional life of the Church (after their original integration in the Mystical Body), come again to mind as proof of the Church's uninterrupted vitality. The course set by Christ's words to Peter and to the other Apostles has not required a change of direction. It is still the only course.

Referring to the Renaissance in Chapter One, we spoke of the increasing marginalization of God and of the gradual transfer of his attributes to man. In this we detected less the process of secularization than the conquest of humanism, indeed we identified it as its essence. From the seventeenth century to the present this has been the main line of force of intellectual history, culminating in Hegel and the post-Hegelians whose legion has not ceased to fill the avenues of culture to this day. It is easy to perceive now in retrospect that this line was bound to penetrate in the Church also, for reasons adduced in all three chapters.

The question we asked earlier concerned the position of the Christian in today's world. In the conclusion of this essay we must address ourselves to a larger problem, the position of the Christian religion. Looking about ourselves without illusion, we may begin by granting Dietrich Bonhoeffer the central thesis of his query: It seems that in the eyes of "modern man," or at least in the eyes of those who speak for him and shape his ideas

a) evil is actually diminishing in the world, and

b) the power to do good is growing in man's hands. Both points may be a thousand times refuted by facts and by those who see the evil face to face—the Russian dissidents and exiles come to mind, but only as the most recent ones—yet perhaps the most potent—humanist—myth today is the one contained in the above points. It is thus logical enough for a Bonhoeffer to conclude that things appear as if God wanted to efface himself from the memory, and certainly from the actions, of mankind. This statement, the approximate Christian equivalent of Nietzsche's "God is dead!" can only be understood as signaling the transfer to man of God's attributes. It means the coming of the post-Christian era, the era of Man.

The signs are so many, they are so evident at every step, that contradicting them seems like the lifting of an enormous block of stone with one's bare hands. At the same time, it is just as evident that Humanism, the cult of man, is incapable of pushing its own weak shoulders under the stone slab and even momentarily to sustain its weight. The dominant experience of several generations is not that a new religion is taking shape under their eyes, but that there is simply *nothing:* After the death of God, man is dead too. In this sense, the post-Christian age may just as well be called the post-humanist age too, since it appears that humanism is unable to refecundate either its ideological or its technological alternative in the spiritually lunar landscape which has become ours.

But here again, as in the case of previously discussed issues, the confrontation between Christianity and Humanism turns out to the former's advantage. For a Hegelian, such a statement is meaningless, antidialectical, antihistorical; a phase in history cannot be brought back, one cannot return to earlier self-manifestations of the World Spirit. This belief is shared by the Christian Hegelians and their intellectual cohorts, whether Teilhard de Chardin, Hans Küng or Karl Rahner. But let us bear in mind that they are Hegelians *because* they do not recognize that Christianity is not a phase in history; in other words, if they are not actually negators of transcendence, they are mentally uncomfortable with it, as, in a sense, Joachim was too.

Not being Hegelians, we are not bound by the rules of everunravelling dialectics: We simply do not know what it is "a return to an earlier phase." Time as such cannot be reversed (or, rather, our measuring of it, the clock), that is true, and styles constantly change; but religious truth is not measured by the historical clock; it possesses validity beyond temporal vicissitudes. It is different with Humanism. Although it may impress the mentality of an epoch, it is not able to build, even to preserve, a civilization. Humanism is experienced today in two ways:

a) as an interregnum, a question mark between two civilizations, a period of confusion, distress and aimlessness, kept alive not by its own creativeness, but by the parallel survival of traditional beliefs and convictions which steady the contemporary human being under whose feet Humanism as such is quicksand; and

b) as a dry ideology by itself, but which tolerates, even breeds monstruous ideologies and behaviors, destructive of human dignity, contemptuous of reason, prompter of animality in all its forms.[14]

Thus, humanism should be regarded as a transition from a civilization with a strong, religion-inspired sense of reality, to an anticivilization where man's worst urges are allowed free course, in view of no other purpose than more pleasure, more hedonism, more drifting in the material and the moral universe. In the general disaffection from all realities which must guide and surround human life for man to see a meaning in existence, the political, cultural, and ethical space in which he continues living inevitably narrows to only two main areas of interest: sex and blood. What is called the present infatuation with pornography and violence is thus neither an infatuation, that is, a capricious choice, nor present, that is limited in duration. Sex and blood mark logically the end of a humanist civilization; they are its necessary outcome. The emphasis on reducing all things to man leads to the ultimate reduction: to the animalistic in man. This may be covered up by sophistication, science, modern life-style or other things, the animalistic character of it is the same. In school it is called real-life education, ultimately sex-education; in cultural life it is called the bold uncovering of life-as-it-is; in the Church it is called the permanent search for Jesus by the autonomous man; and so on. From an easy-going "civilization of play" conceived as the postwar relaxation of mores, a kind of anti-puritanic reaction, a supposedly freer examination of the facts of life, etc., we have switched to the heavier, deadlier side of sin: mass-murder of unborn children, the surviving child's bodily and mental corruption in school,[15] the live showing by the media of executions, hold-ups, atrocities, even theologians encouraging hatred, murder and removal of all restraint.[16]

For man in quest of meaning and of decent life forms, humanism is not an option, it is moral and spiritual suicide. Confrontation between it and religion creates a false alternative: There has never been a society resting on "humanistic" values, only, as said before, a liquidation of society which was slowed down by still lingering Christian values. Thus, there is not even a choice between religion and Humanism. It is easy to discourse learnedly about various models of society, as if the planners had in front of them spare parts from which to put together a machine. What they lack is a model so transcending man that no ideology or mechanism may be the result of its imitation. For in the face of all possible humanisms and their glorification of man, it is profoundly true that "man on his own does not know who he is. He lacks the authentic prototype of humanity. He lacks the true Son of God: a living model for the true man," the ground for the only authentic Humanism.[17]

Footnotes to Chapter Three.

1. *National Catholic Register,* April 17, 1977. Italics in the original.

2. Joachim displayed the same impatience vis-à-vis what he called the "second period," that of the Gospel of Jesus Christ, and pushed forward to the Third Age.

3. After Joachim's and Comte's influence, here we find Bonhoeffer's thesis that God wants us in the twentieth century to emancipate ourselves from his tutelage and come of age in a Godless world.

4. "Croire dans un monde scientifique" (Belief in an age of science), a course of five lectures, published in 1974 by the Ed. du Cerf. Second edition, 1975.

5. "If nothing happens to moderate this trend . . .," the Pope said in January, 1970. Now, seven years later, we still find that nothing happened.

6. Various scholars, H. I. Marrou, Simone Petrement, etc., suggest possible identifications with more or less plausibility.

7. Before the ninth great persecution, that of Emperor Decius in A.D. 250, the Emperor Alexander Severus had placed a figure of Christ in his private chapel, next to other gods worshipped in the Empire. Cca 235 A.D.

8. *On Being a Christian,* Doubleday, 1976, 720 pages.

9. These remedial excursions into inhumanity may be evaluated by the reaction they meet: The Bolivian peasants captured Guevara and handed him over to the authorities; Mrs. Gandhi, apostle of forced sterilization, was enthusiastically voted out of office in March, 1977.

10. The same reasons motivated many Protestants up till the present to become converts to Catholicism.

11. A third point might be added, often made by the great Belgian philosopher, Marcel De Corte, namely that the transfer of faith leaves intact the sacerdotal fervor, so that the fervent ex-priest becomes a fanatic secularist, an ideologue or a humanist,

a persecutor of his earlier brothers and sisters in faith. One should remember a passage in Bernanos' writings, that sounded too absurd and shocking at the time: "One day I may be shot down by a bolshevik priest!"

12. The limits that Yves Congar sets to the "reformable" are drawn by him along the line of historical accretions. These history-imposed accretions, writes Congar, should not be absolutized since they do not belong to the essence of Christianity. On the other hand, belonging to the essence are: the repository of apostolic faith, the sacraments, magisterium and priesthood. *Vraie et fausse réforme dans l'Eglise,* pp. 52, 146.

13. It is assumed here, however, that all human issues have a spiritual resonance, cause and effect. Whether revolutions (or agrarian reforms) are good things or bad, are ultimately spiritual problems too. As the early French socialist (and atheist) Proudhon, declared with astonishment but with a remarkable intellectual honesty, all mundane issues have theological roots. What the Church calls prudential judgment is the all-important *distance* existing between a careful and necessarily general formulation, and the hic et nunc character of the issue with its unforeseeable contingencies.

14. Recent "humanistic" textbooks and filmstrips and class experiments show the trend towards animality. Eskimo life is shown to little children, stressing the exposure of the old and impotent to die alone on an ice floe; a child is shown beating a seagull to death; small children participate in a game where they are supposed to *be* (not just *play*) baboons; they are told that there is no good and evil, expediency is to be followed; the many kinds of sensory therapies, now introduced to church classes also, suggest that people should touch each other, ultimately to be promiscuous. It is no longer *mens sana in corpore sano;* it is now the submission of both body and mind to the flux of lost identity, leading to sensuous life and obscenity.

15. I have in front of me a copy of the parents' advertisement, "What is in the West Virginia Textbooks?" *Charleston Gazette,* November 14, 1974. In the passages reprinted from textbooks for grade and high school students across the United States, obsenity competes with vulgarity, blasphemy with swear words,

primitive taste with hatred, incitement to violence with contempt for law, for love, for religion.

16. Under the title "The Church, 1976," the *Informations Catholiques Internationales,* a semiofficial Church publication in Paris, run by "progressive Catholics," exalts man liberated from all conditions: economic, political, cultural. "The core of the Gospels is freedom, all appeal should have as its goal the liberation of man, a radical transformation of society." The same publication shows pictures of "liberated" priests, nuns, children—in communist Poland and communist Vietnam. "The Church has enjoyed until now," runs the commentary, "the favor of established authorities. The hour of nakedness for the Church has struck." March 15, 1977.

17. Pope Paul's homily on Christmas Day, 1969.

Index of Names

Adickes, E., 61f
Agrippa, v. N., 23, 80, 82
Alessandri, J., 121f
Allende, S., 121f
Alexander Severus, 165f
Ambrose, St., 117
Aristotle, 19, 20, 67, 83
Ars, Curé d, 152
Arius, 6, 58f, 70
Augustine, St., 5, 27, 54, 59f,
   61f, 85, 114, 117, 142
Augustus, 49
Averroes, 23

Bacon, of V., 60f
Bakunin, N., 37
Barth, K., 84
Baum, G., 51
Bayle, P., 32
Bembo, Card., 158
Benedict, St., 117
Bengel, J. A., 133, 135
Berdyaev, N., 99
Bernard, St., 17, 141
Bernanos, G., 166f
Berulle, Card., 81
Bloch, E., 45
Blumhardt, Chr., 110
Bodin, J., 30, 31, 35, 60f
Boehmer, H., 78
Boissier, G., 58f
Bonhoeffer, D., 71, 91, 92, 93,
   95, 99, 100, 162, 165f
Bossuet, B., 86
Bouyer, L., 28
Brehier, E., 5
Bruno, G., 80
Bultmann, R., 50, 51, 56, 61f
Busson, H., 118f, 119f

Buonaiuti, E., 16, 45
Burckhardt, J., 37, 38

Calvin, J., 82, 84, 120f
Camara, H., 120f
Camus, A., 37, 38
Capitan, 84
Casaubon, I., 59f
Caspari, 61f
Cassirer, E., 60f
Celsus, 7, 8
Chou En-lai, 104
Cicero, 22
Clavel, M., 139
Cohn, N., 11
Colet, F., 106
Comte, A., 15, 34, 39, 40, 73,
   75, 125, 127, 165f
Congar, Y., 52, 135, 159, 166f
Condillac, E., 41
Condorcet, A. N., 15, 37
Constantine, 37
Cserhati, J., 113
Cullmann, O., 108, 109, 118f
Cusanus, N., 18, 19, 20, 21, 22,
   24, 25, 26, 27, 28, 30, 33, 42,
   47, 59f, 80, 81, 125, 142,
   151, 157

Dante, A., 54, 76
Darwin, Ch., 47
Decius, 165f
De Corte, M., 165f
Deleage, 96
Denys, the Areopagite, 19
Descartes, R., 21, 32, 33, 60f,
   85, 86, 90, 103, 105, 116,
   119f, 121f
Dewey, J., 38, 90